"Is it so nice as all that?" asked the Mole.

"Nice? It's the only thing, . . . there is nothing—absolutely nothing—half so much worth doing as simply messing about. Nothing seems really to matter, that's the charm of it. Whether you get away, or whether you don't; whether you arrive at your destination or whether you reach somewhere else, or whether you never get anywhere at all, you're always busy, and you never do anything in particular; and when you've done it there's always something else to do, and you can do it if you like, but you'd much better not."

The Wind In the Willows
Kenneth Grahame

Courtesy of Charles Scribner's Sons

GYPSYING AFTER 40

A Guide to Adventure & Self-Discovery

by
Robert W. Harris

Edited by
Toni Drew

Cover and Illustrations by
Brian Hough

Designed by
Mary Shapiro

TO Megan and MCFL

Published by John Muir Publications
P.O. Box 613
Santa Fe, New Mexico 87501

Printed in the United States of America

First Edition, September 1987

Library of Congress Catalog Number 87-042768

Distributed to the trade by W.W. Norton & Co.
New York, NY

ISBN 0-912528-71-0

TABLE OF CONTENTS

PROLOGUE: A TRAVELER'S CONFESSION

Threats

N ikos Kazantzakis confessed: *"My life's greatest benefactors have been journeys and dreams." In my experience, dreams direct my travels and travel feeds my dreams. I'm not a hero with great deeds in my quiver; I am an ordinary man who settled for "prosperity and a woman's embrace" along with the comfort of children and acceptance in a tame society. When travel finally took command of my life, extraordinary events shook the core of my being. In fact, my ordinary life was threatened.*

Fiery experiences burned my soul time and again: 10th century religious frescoes leapt at me with unimaginable intensity and anguish; their frightening images clawed at my guts. On the other side of things, tranquil Renaissance paintings assured me of the heavenly realm I yearned for but could not accept; regal palaces rose in cruel splendor to speak of awesome power; huge cities spread before me as monuments of man's capacities for excellence and evil. But the greatest experiences—and I remain powerfully affected—were at holy sites where men commune with the pantheon of gods.

Discovery

For me, travel-after-forty is a pilgrimage. I began to question my long-held beliefs about Good and Evil, Passivity and Aggression, God and Mankind. Some daemon planned my itinerary and led me to specific sites where I was offered unique revelations. Each of us holds to a creed no matter how poorly articulated; my pilgrimage exposed my creed so that, at last, I could examine it and was commended to "choose how you will be, who you will be, what gods you worship!"

Romanesque Frescoes

Through no accident I was directed to the Barcelona Art Museum of Catalonia in Spain. It is devoted to 10th century church frescoes. I entered a huge space in which bright lights focused on a weird collection of saints and devils and "other-worldly" beings. They stared down at me threateningly. Painted in assertive outlines to emphasize omniscience, peering from a backdrop of stars, clouds and angels with huge wings to affirm their power and majesty, they frightened me with their intensity and gigantic size. Looming down was a twenty-foot-tall Christ whose head reached high into the vault forty feet above. Lightning radiated from its head and a swarm of giant angels projected furious anger and guilt.

Saints were tortured—sawn in half, shrieking in agony, their faces contorted with large eyes staring directly at me, accusingly. Wall after wall hung with frescoes depicting savage scenes more horrific than any of my imaginings—more violent, and somehow more real. They had a clear message: I and all others transgress against holy law and continue to live in abominable ways. I stood feeling accused, judged and condemned.

Italian Perfection

When I gazed on the paintings of Fra Angelico in Florence, I saw evil totally subdued—pinned captive under the feet of angels. God and His saints were triumphant, serene victors in the battle for life. The clear pigments—vermillion and fresh morning-sky blue depict serene madonnas and helpful angels frozen in time before dream-world landscapes. The polished, ivory countenances of men and women, apostles and saints occupied a rational, perfected world untainted by trouble and torture. Though warmed and seduced by Angelico's vision, I could not accept it when it meant renouncing the fuller reality I'd come to know.

Fra Lippo's View

It was Fra Lippo Lippi's paintings that held a vision I could match with my life. Lippi's Madonnas depict women whose human beauty is uplifted, exalted and glowing with the satisfaction over the child she has borne.

Lippi painted human values—the family, intellect, emotional warmth, the joy of children, the wonder of generation—and suffused these scenes with sacred light. In a painting central to his work, the Madonna is a beautiful mother surrounded by a flock of children; Jesus is an alert child with his hand extended to the viewer; angels are scallywag Italian kids with laughter lighting their faces. One of them faces us and there's no denying his query as he points to his new Brother and asks straight on: "Can you beat that?"

I'm drawn into Lippi's scenes as the father of children he might well have used as models, and as a participant in the family that we call Holy. He invites me to a crisis where I lay my human qualities on an altar praying that they be transformed. I often returned to the Uffizzi Galleries in Florence to stand transfixed before Lippi's work. He seemed to say to me: "Take what you are. With all the betrayals of trust, the failure to rise to your highest potential, the uncertainties, the fears for your flesh—take all these and accept them as sacred materials to be wrought anew."

A Greek Ghost

My pilgrimage led to Lindos, Rhodes. I climbed the steep path to the high promontory washed on three sides by the Mediterranean far below. At the top are remains of a Greek temple: hardly more than a few broad marble steps and a paved floor, where slender columns rise magnificently to support short lintel stones silhouetted against a startling blue sky. Something compelled me to step rashly into the sacred precinct, while an equally strong urge warned me to stay back. Up here the winds moaned, and several hundred feet below the sea growled. I had done the unthinkable, going into the sanctuary; the moan and the growl blended into a single unearthly cry warning me to retreat. I moved outside.

I knew that like all Greek temples, Lindos was designed as the welcoming home for a god to enter and inhabit; earthly suppliants were to stand outside. The architect's first task was to find the god's favorite setting. His second task was to erect a perfect temple on that

11

spot. The architect of the Temple of Athena in Lindos met with uncommon success: the god had clearly entered, dwelt, and lingered for more than two thousand years.

High on the promontory, standing at a distance from the holy temple, my heart raced with a strange excitement. The dweller in that temple was a furious god who demanded excellence, the highest achievement in building His home, the greatest perceptive clarity. This vision challenged my soft, gentle, ineffectual sense of a Supreme Being.

Pagan Places

During my travels, I gradually let go of the sharp distinction between Judaeo-Christian figures and the "pagan" figures of older religions. Though the sacred signs are different, I discern the same God behind them: a Creative Force in many guises, appearing throughout the ages to disparate peoples with common need. I experienced the presence of dynamic agencies dwelling in certain places, occupying shrines, grottoes, temples, springs and groves.

On one occasion, a simple thirst drove me into a hand-cut tunnel to a flowing spring at the heart of Ibiza Island, Spain. Carved into the vaulted roof of the tunnel were geometric symbols which were colored with mineral pigments. This set the place apart as a sacred shrine. Tradition says Phoenician sailors worshiped here when they came ashore to replenish their water casks. Kneeling to scoop a handful of water, I began to shake; I drank deeply and a great calm took hold of me—a feminine, gentling presence was clearly at hand. Was it Tanit, the goddess who was worshipped here in prehistoric times? In the weeks we remained on the island, I went often to the sacred spring to receive many levels of refreshment.

The Sacred Moment

Now when my wife, Megan, and I visit a shrine, we expect to become entangled in the sacred Moment. This happened at the "Wailing Wall" in Jerusalem—the only remains of Solomon's temple—at the

Bar-Mitzvah of a group of Jewish boys.

The limestone rose from a sunken court constructed of carefully fitted stones. It functions as retaining wall for the elevated plaza called "Temple Mount." Here Solomon built his temple as a symbol of Hebrew unity, and two thousand years ago the Romans tore it down. The Jews deep desire to rebuild it is ironic because the mount is occupied by, and central to, Moslem worship, and no Jew can stride in the plaza above as it is off-limits to them. The entrance ramp is guarded against terrorists by Israeli soldiers carrying automatic weapons.

We stood a little way off to watch the proceedings. Hasidim Rabbis in big black hats, side curls dangling to their shoulders, moved among the group at the Wall as guides and masters of ceremony. The boys' fathers, in flowing white prayer shawls and black yarmulkes, stood near the wall rocking back and forth in the jerky motions of their prayer. The boys, in matching finery, joined in the same ritual prayers as their fathers. Drummers hammered out a hypnotic rhythm. A ram's horn bleat signalled the men to raise the boys to their shoulders and begin to circle and dance. The prayer chanting rose to a wail until a second bleat signalled. At that, everything—drums, motions, wail—suddenly stopped.

Below the wall there was an utter silence and stillness—as quiet as the end of the world. A moment later, a cry rose, a scream, an eons-old pain shifting into a howl. The tremulous scream rocked the space. The spectators stood rigid with alarm. Had there been a terrorist attack? The fluttering wail increased as it was taken up by all the participants who threw their hands in the air and began to leap and twirl in rapturous, crazy dancing. The scene recalled to us primitive tribesmen, uninhibited madmen. We watched as the ordeal unwound, the boys stood on the ground once more, the wailing ceased. The plaza quieted as men and boys clasped and kissed the unyielding stone. We imagined that we heard the promises they made, the vows vowed.

Never before had we witnessed such an extreme display of devotion, such eruption of emotion. We wondered if we would ever fulfill so profoundly the intrinsic thrust of our own historical and religious roots.

13

Could we ever abandon ourselves so completely in such a ritual? We were witness to the strength of faith required to forge a nation.

Peacefulness Along The Galilee

A few days later we strolled along the Sea of Galilee to a restored church on the shore where the Great Fisherman appeared to His disciples after His Resurrection. Tradition says that He cooked a meal for them here.

Just off the chancel, a small bare room had been set aside for quiet meditation. A vase of wild flowers formed the only decoration and focus. Fresh air wafting through a window brought in the only incense. Silently, with our eyes closed, we sat and waited. Nothing disturbed the quiet: no solemn sermon, no jubilant dancing, no wails. Thick walls protected us from distractions. Gently, a presence filled the room and lingered; we were overcome with a sense of peace. With no need to exclaim nor even speak of this experience, we quietly rose and left with a blessing which now hovers over all our Gypsy adventures.

THE GYPSY CHALLENGE

How It Began For Us

"I just don't see how you do it," said my brother-in-law as he lounged in the cockpit of our boat. "Here you are sitting in the sunshine, on this sailboat, in this fantastic port, on an island in the Mediterranean." He waved at the surrounding view: the little stone houses built down to the water's edge, the fishing boats clutched together at the stone quay, their wheel-houses painted orange, blue and green. Around the harbor, hills rose to form a wall of green forests and fields of flowers waved gently in the breeze. The scent of pine drifted to the deck to mingle with the seaweed and fish net smells. A clear blue sky was washed by a golden sun. It could not have been a more peaceful nor a more perfect spot in which to linger.

"Whadya mean, how do we do it?" I knew what he meant, but I wanted him to say it.

"Well. . .you took off two years ago, got this boat. . .ah. . . the cost and all. You know what I mean." That was too much for me. Here was this guy who wore hand-stitched, three-piece suits, drove a Bentley, jetted around checking on his business, never going anywhere or doing anything other than first class. And he was asking me, the poor relation, how I did it!

"Look, what did this boat cost?" he queried. When I answered, he exploded, "You're kidding! That can't be right. Why the boat yard charged me almost that much to get my little launch ready for the season. And that was only for putting on a coat of paint and varnishing the deck. Come on. What did it really cost?"

"That's all the money Megan and I have in it. Practically all we've got. We bought the old hull, wood and tools to repair it, a few new fittings and paid for one haul-out. Then there was

17

paint." I could have told him about the nine months of back-breaking work, about the help our sons and their girlfriends gave us.

I could have told him that part of the cost was in nights of troubled sleep twitching with fatigue. Or described the hours bargaining for an old winch that had been bolted to a half-sunken wreck, but. . .why bother. Besides, looking back on it all. . .it was fun.

We wanted to be Gypsies. We had stopped what we had been doing and. . .left. What he really wanted to know was how anyone could leave his work and home and travel overseas without knowing anything about what he would find, how much it would cost, or how long he would stay. How in the world could you just pull up roots and take off?

He wasn't the only one to ask. How did we decide? Hadn't we thought we were too old? Too poor? What about the future? Weren't we avoiding responsibility? What did our kids think about it? What would we do when we had to face up to. . .and here they all ran out of steam. "Well," we asked, "face up to what?"

How could I tell my fine relative and all the others how we had decided. Maybe it happened like this:

We were sitting at breakfast, our two younger sons were already off to school and I, as usual, was eating too fast in a rush to get to the office. There was a contract to review and overdue plans to finish.

"Will you be home early for supper?"

"Early? Probably not. I have to finish a set of plans and redo some preliminaries and. . .I guess I'd better grab a hamburger and put in a couple of late hours. You go on without me. Ouch!" I'd scalded myself with hot coffee.

"Why don't you slow down?"

What? Me slow down? How could I slow down when I always felt that I was forever behind schedule. Here I was in a perpetual hurry and my wife wanted me to slow down. To humor her, I leaned back in the chair in an attitude of relaxation. "How's this?"

"Fine. Only you're just acting. You really do need to pause once in awhile, take a look at how things are going. I really do mean. . .," and here she herself paused as if to let the idea sink in. . ."s. . .l. . .o. . .w   d. . .o. . .w. . .n."

Each time she repeated it, the "slow down" acted like an incantation, like a hypnotist saying: "You. . .are. . .going. . . to. . .s·l·e·e·p." I started to reach again for the hot cup of coffee, then her incantation did its thing. I paused. I stopped in mid-movement and waited. Her words, "slow down," suddenly hit the key. Something clicked like a lock springing open. Something did open: a door swung through a small arc letting in light. . .from beyond. Unexpectedly, every muscle let go, tensions eased while mentally I reached out towards that door and that light.

"Slow down? How do I do that? I wonder? Suppose we were to, well. . .close up shop. . .and get away for awhile? Get away for a few months. . .maybe longer, a year, say?" I watched her eyes widen as I spoke. "We could do that. . .some way," I ended lamely.

With a whir I could hear the old imagination begin to work on this idea of slowing down, of getting away for a year. A year in which to go slower and start thinking things out. "Let's see," I began to calculate, "we could start saving right now. Or better yet, think what we would save if we weren't living in this house and operating the office. There wouldn't be the utility payments. Hmm, hmm. . .think of what our monthly phone bill is; we could save all that." I reached for some paper and a pencil and began to write down figures of our monthly outlays. Megan said nothing.

"And if I closed the office, I would no longer need an accountant, a lawyer, expensive trips. Hmm. . .and without income, there'd be no income taxes." It must have been unusually strong coffee, because there I sat subtracting away, cutting down fixed monthly outlays, reducing and reducing until it appeared that it would cost us absolutely nothing to live. Somehow.

Scribbling madly, I added all the costs of doing business, of living in a house, of making a presentable appearance. And what about entertaining? In a long pent-up frustration with inflation, I kept adding things we would no longer need to buy or pay for. There had been too little money and too little time with my wife, children and friends.

This was a great game; just add and add all the costs of things we could do without if we weren't living at home, operating an office, keeping-up-with-the-Joneses. Totalled and grand totalled and grand, grand totalled it came to a whopping big amount.

"Aren't you forgetting something?" Megan asked as calmly as talking to a three year old in a tantrum, throwing out his toys.

"Forget? Don't think I have. Added all up, we could save, let's see. . .about. . .nope. You're right, I did forget something, I forgot to add the. . .why it makes it even bigger." I could feel my serious-sincere look coming over me, "Do you know, by cutting out all those things we could save. . .," and here I caught my breath. Her look had finally penetrated my delirium, "You mean, what would being some place else cost?"

"Yes. Just a little thing like that. Your big total needs a little subtracting. And you've been subtracting from zero, from no income. How do you do that?" She started ringing down the curtain on one of my best hot-house dramas to date. If we went someplace else we would have to rent a house. "And food and other things. . .," she said but started to slow down when she saw my face collapse.

"But dearest, the Indians didn't have those expenses and they roamed all over the plains. And Gypsies?" Here I knew

I was playing a dirty card, since from the first day, first hour that we'd met, I knew I had a Gypsy on my hands. She usually wore big circle earrings and full skirts with ruffles, a low cut blouse, lots of bangly jewelry and sandals on her feet. And the few times we had managed to sneak off for a week or so, she radiated. Even now with three sons, two grandchildren and grey wisps in her hair, thinking about a trip turned her into a girl again.

"Gypsies? You mean we could be Gypsies?" Her practical, good homemaker look started dissolving while her eyes focused somewhere about a zillion miles away.

I waited, watching in wonderment as her face went through changes: wrinkles smoothed, her head lifted as if seeing over an invisible wall blocking the sight from a beautiful view, a view over sparkling seas, down flower-decked roads, along tree-lined canals, up steps to Italian, French, Greek villages. Slowly she rose from the table to walk to the window trying to see what her mind was conjuring. "Maybe we could."

"What about selling the rental property we own?" I suggested. "That would bring in something. We've nearly paid off the mortgage."

"Sure," she said dreamily.

"And we could sell the cars," I egged her on, holding my breath hoping the moment would not pass.

"I could cash in that old insurance policy my father started when I was a child and I've been paying for all these years. And suppose we cancelled your two policies? Do we need them anymore? I've been wanting to sell some furniture and a couple of rugs. You know how antiques have gone up in price recently." She sat at the table and looked at my scribbled figures and the total and then, taking a clean sheet of paper started afresh.

Here she became sharp, practical, "Forget all that saving as if it were income. It isn't. Let's figure what it would cost if, just if, we took off for Europe some cheap way and then bought a tent or a camper and. . .," she stopped, startled and looked up at me. "Do you really mean it? Do you really want to be a Gypsy?"

Unusual Business

Many of us have unfinished business with life; after-forty is a good time to work on it. As with cleaning up the garage, a certain ruthlessness is required. A lot of just plain unidentifiable "stuff" has to be moved out to clear space for a good clear vision of what is most important. Changing stride in mid-life is mind-breaking labor, yet it renews and refreshes.

We had precious little time left to catch up with old dreams so we decided to change all that and heed Thoreau's advice: ". . . if one advances confidently in the direction of his dreams, and endeavors to live the life which he has imagined, he will meet with success unexpected in common hours."

We packed up and set off to travel for a year in Greece with the foolish assurance we knew what we wanted and what we were doing. It took a great deal of pain and anguish to learn how to go about "advancing" more easily. Yet we met with so much success on our first journey that three years after returning home we left again for an even longer adventure. And we have done so again and again.

Suffering and Shifts

You, too, may suffer from living with unfinished business, curiosity about distant places, fascination with exotic people, passion to see what's on the other side of the mountain and lust to satisfy these urges. In this book we want to feed that passion and tell you how to fulfill your dreams. You won't be alone since thousands of people make long-term travel their main mode of existence and awake each morning as if it were

22

the shining first day of their lives. You'll meet some of them in these pages and more of them in secluded camps in cool woods, under a tent in hot deserts or shopping in native markets. They are vitally alive and constantly burst with fresh enthusiasms. They glow with new personalities created by the challenges of their adventures.

The Gypsy life affords you the time to cavort with nature, dive into deep wells of reading, warm the fires of friendship, wrestle with meditations. The road is open so you can choose the world you wish and people it with giants, fill it with accomplishments; or you can simplify your existence like a mystic. And always a full measure of the unexpected arises to keep you on your toes, to intrigue, amuse and stretch you.

Too Old?

Some people think themselves too old to take up Gypsying. This may be true; many thirty year olds become so immobile, so immune to new experiences and so uninterested in adventure that, yes, they are too old. But if you can toddle along at a reasonable pace and have a curiosity that has never been satisfied, you are certainly not too old to start down the Gypsy trail.

Our friend, Mio, was seventy when she and another lady of a mere sixty years determined to go to Spain. They chose a slow boat as the best way and this gave them days of perfect cruising. Their first stop was Madeira, Portugal, where all the passengers disembarked for a day of sightseeing. Here in the Atlantic, our "young-old friend" discovered a place fitting a young girl's vision of heaven: an island rising as a mountain from the sea covered with everblooming flowers, an island with only one season—perpetual Spring.

A few hours before they were to go back to the boat they decided to stop for tea at a resort hotel. As they sat down, Mio glanced around to discover at the next table a friend she hadn't seen in twenty years.

"Ed! What are you doing here?"

He turned and with his one good eye stared back finally realizing who she was. "By golly. You here! When did you come?" His face broke into a smile that bridged all the years gone by.

"I'm not really here," she said. "This is just a day's stopover and our boat is taking us on to Spain. But I do like it here, it's beautiful. . . I wish I could stay."

"Why not stay?" he shot back. "I've been here eight years and it's perfect."

Mio turning to her just-sixty companion, shrugged a question. An hour later, she had arranged with the boat's steward to send their luggage ashore. Years later, she was still thrilled with her decision to stay. She never did go to Spain.

Who's Irresponsible?

Of course plenty of people will attempt to discourage you from dropping everything to become a Gypsy: relatives, friends, even people whom you've met casually at parties. They will ask "Isn't this the wrong decision? Are you sure about this? Aren't you afraid of the cost? What will your kids think? Don't they still need you? What about the future? How in the world can you just pull up roots and take off? What's the matter? Is your business failing? Your marriage?"

You'll learn Gypsying is NOT dropping out: Gypsying helps you join IN the mainstream of living internationally, making friends and enjoying people far from your neighborhood.

Do you love your work? Stopping for a time gives you the unrivaled opportunity to acquire new perspectives, to retreat. When you return, you will have rediscovered the simple delight in your chosen work, the thrills of younger days.

If you love being a homemaker, you will discover the biggest challenge of your life making a home in the tight spaces of a camping van or on a moving, pitching boat. You'll observe what native people eat, how they concoct special recipes from the simplest ingredients, and work at almost forgotten handicrafts. Homemakers broaden, deepen and perfect their skills.

When It's Time

The vision of Gypsying strikes hard when your career and hopes have reached an anticipated level of success and the once distant challenge has become reality. The lure of starting a new life strikes again when retirement beckons. At such times we need to step out towards vital new directions. Listen carefully to that voice whispering inside you. It begs you to take risks, start afresh, and seek new vistas.

Cutting The Anchor Rope

"Gypsying sounds wonderful," you say. "But what's the price?" The true price is measured not in money, but in the pain of relinquishing your current attitudes and habits of thought. There is no avoiding it. Gypsying will force you to come face to face with yourself.

LESSONS FROM GYPSYING

Changes In Us

We left home, bought a van, headed down the open road, and camped under the stars. We lived among people whose laws and customs were different from ours. Of necessity we continually adapted to their customs, learned their languages and responded to their cultures. Despite our continual adaptations we developed a new style that is distinctly our own. Inside our rejuvenated bodies a fresh reality brewed.

We began our Gypsy adventure with the intention to retreat from the world and see some sights. Yet along the way the strong personal character and dignity of people as they live day-to-day became the focus of our travels. We dumped a lot of attitudes about what was important, what we thought of as principles and as the "right" manner of living. Our travels taught us to prize openness, to adapt to a wide variety of living conditions, to accept the suspicious condition of being "foreigners" ourselves.

This new life put us in touch with our earthiness and exuberance. We left our settled way behind with its house, sedentary pursuits and constant hankering after money. We lived closer to rough weather and discomfort. We became sensitized to seasons and nature. We may have looked purposeless because we moved about with no particular plan. Compared to our former life, our new one seemed rootless, homeless and adrift. But we were not rootless; we discovered an inner place that went right along with us wherever we traveled. We were not vagabonds; we found an enduring domesticity that enabled us to feel at home everywhere. We were far from being adrift; our life flowed purposefully from a profound centeredness.

We left home in pursuit of a dream. It was a daring thing

to do because we did not really know what our inner resources were. The discovery of supple, but strong inner selves gave us the flexibility to enjoy the nomadic life with an openness akin to authentic Gypsies.

Genuine Gypsies

Before our travels began, we regarded Gypsies as con-artists: immoral and unclean. But our new estate forced us to reconsider our prejudice. Our worries diminished and our laughter erupted often. We began to take troubles in stride. When we arrived at a new place, we were eager to interact. Poetry and beauty became infinitely more important to us than security. In no way did we feel like con-artists. And we definitely felt clean.

We revised our picture of Gypsies when our nomadic existence gave us a window to theirs. Despite difficult times and setbacks, their life is punctuated with joy and laughter. They have persisted for centuries in spite of hostility, slavery and massacre. In the process of dealing with harsh realities they have become fierce, passionate, wily, swift and wise. They maintain a style of affectionate warmth in their close-knit families. Among Gypsies you can hear the shouts of children, jingle of jewelry and lilt of song. They have an unquenchable vitality. We know of course that we are not real Gypsies, and you will never be a real Gypsy either. We have chosen these champions of Living Free as our guide because they demonstrate that LIFE CAN BE FUN.

Identity Crisis

I had a hellishly hard time shedding my old self-image. I remember our introductory Gypsying. We lived in a remote farmhouse on a small island in Greece. During the first nights I slept fitfully with only the gentle thrumming of crickets as lullaby. About three each morning the shrill ringing of a nonexistent telephone shattered my slumbers and summoned me to work. Sitting bolt upright, I'd remember the personal identity that went with those anxious summons. My old image didn't want to let go.

As that self-image began to loosen, I'd find myself frightened. Early in the morning I'd rush through washing up and dressing as if headed for an appointment at the office. Then I'd stop and realize there wasn't any impending activity that had to be performed. I alone could pick and choose whether to go swim or walk or read or lounge around. No one was waiting for me to do anything. Indeed, it was no longer necessary to answer to anyone. Then the shudders began.

It took time to drop the old me and even more time to find the new me. New interests gained my attention. The arrival of dawn, changes in weather, movement in clouds, the ever-shifting face of the sea all became important to me. The goings-on around me—insects moving, animals browsing, farmers harvesting—became spectacles. My bruised ego decreased in importance while rich curiosity and heightened awareness increased.

My relationship with my wife underwent dramatic shifts until a fantastic new level of respect and love burst forth.

The true personalities of my children came into focus; at last I knew them as the great beings I was privileged to share my life with.

Life really began again for me after forty.

Travel As Teacher

At a party in our van one night, we were sharing anecdotes and adventures when a young Dutchman spoke up. "You know, travel changes you, not just a little but completely. You can never return to being what you were before." That stopped

the conversation while each of us thought about personal changes that we had undergone. We thought of the times we had resisted change and tried to crawl back into our shells. We confessed that it had been hard and taken time to accept the lessons. We agreed that the Gypsy life is risky and sometimes scary; yet not one of us regretted the changes that this lifestyle has wrought. We felt richer, more related, healthier and happier.

Identity Shifts

It is difficult for people in the second half of their life to weather an identity crisis, because we are already so developed. But this crisis occurs whether we stay at home, move to a new house or state, switch jobs, have an affair or go Gypsying.

Encounters Teach

We brought our old sailboat into a small Spanish fishing port to be rebuilt. The work was going far too slowly, and at last we discovered someone was causing a deliberate slowdown. Word came that the port's chief customs official stood at the heart of the problem. When we went to see him, he admitted he wanted us to go—*marcharse!*

"Fine," I said, "We want to leave more than you want us to. But we can't leave until our boat's ready to sail. You help us get finished, then we'll leave."

He insisted we'd overstayed our legal time. We showed him that we'd recently traveled to France so we had a new visa which allowed us to stay another six months. He glowered and kept insisting we leave. We pointed out that it would be suicide to go to sea in a half-completed boat. He wouldn't listen.

This impasse persisted for weeks. Frustration mounted to the purple-faced, thumping-adrenaline level. Pride was the ultimate issue. He and I each wanted to dominate the situation. The official had all the power in his hands, so he did not need to be reasonable. Finally it dawned on me that my pride was insisting that I be the one in control of the situation, that events proceed according to the rules of my previous world where I was an established professional and petty officials existed to serve me. Rather suddenly, my stiff neck began to loosen and my irritability subsided. I recognized that my insistence on being right and in control was only making the official even more stubborn. I was not the victim; I was the source of the problem!

I went back to the customs office, carefully forgot all my Spanish, mumbled, grinned foolishly. . .and stalled. I met the man's official ranting and raving with a shrug of total incomprehension: "Heh? What's that? Would you say that again? I don't understand you. Would you repeat that? Would you repeat that again? Please, s. . .l. . .o. . .w. . .l. . .y."

To his power play I was responding as a helpless idiot. I appeared to be too dumb to understand what he said. He got furious. For him, this was no longer fun. To speed our departure he went to the boat yard and reversed his previous instructions. "Quickly, speed up the work!"

After that, magical things happened, the boat rebuilding was completed, and we left a month later.

The playacting worked but it left a funny taste in my mouth. I had won the confrontation, but I had lost my certainty. Had I been in the right, had I been clever to have thought of this gimmick? It was his country. He had to solve the problems in his own way. And another thing. . .when acting the fool, a bit of my old assurance had dissolved. I had to admit that the assurance was not much more than a habit, a shell, a baseless mask. My identity shifted from Established American Architect to unidentified human being who would be accepted only on immediate terms. I was learning to live in the now, without my previous reputation. This began to change my expectations of how people would respond to me.

When a French customs official stopped me from doing what I wanted, I slipped immediately into my dumbbell act. To my surprise, the act worked most effectively on me. Instead of seeing a problem, I experienced a human being. He really did have a beautiful moustache! I studied it intently. His eyebrows did express wisdom. The whole encounter shifted from one of frustration to one of friendliness. At this point, the official appeared to change, perhaps because my perception changed. He received a projection of positive affection from me instead of anger. His "no's" turned to "yes's," his frown to a smile. And then we smiled together. A different world opened up; a new reality began for me. I was emerging out the other side of my identity crisis as a person I liked more—healthier, more open and more responsive.

My feelings towards others changed too. The people we hired, the men who should "serve us". . . reversed roles and became honored teachers. When Pablo fashioned metal parts for our boat, I marveled at his inventive genius and learned to copy his patience and concentration. When Raphael repaired the old engine, he apprenticed me, taught me proper tool handling and respect for a machine's potential. Their classroom instilled in me the highest regard for crafts people. We discovered their true value came from personal integrity and dogged determination. With all the concern and skill poured into the rebuilding we finally had a beautiful and seaworthy boat that gave us years of happy sailing. I am finding a new approach to my fellowman, seeing him as a human being with the same temptations and failings as myself, with the same potential for being grand and wonderful. Now I approach people with the belief that every stranger might be a god in disguise.

The Gypsy Viewpoint

What a lesson from real Gypsies! Historically, the Gypsies were subjected to centuries of misrule and murder at the hands of such officials. The Gypsy does not accept defeat, but instead uses his wit and insight to dissolve problems. He rejects the world that you and I sadly look upon and replaces it with a sunny view that most events, most things are created especially for him—bright events brimming with opportunities. It is easy to be victimized, and the traveler, like the Gypsy, is an unprotected mark. He has few legal weapons. Our experience as travelers has taught us to armor ourselves with a positive attitude and a keenly aware body and mind that can flex and transform to meet the world head on. This new protection does not invite exploitation. We do not assume a naive stance, but an open and alert one.

Seeing Without Judging

The habit of seeing people as OBJECTS is a sure way to dismiss what is before our eyes and bypass the moment. When we dismiss someone, we miss the NOW and every valuable interaction that goes with it.

Travel provides a precious opportunity for faulty vision to clear. Constant moving among new people and experiences makes it hard to issue simple condemnations based on old classifications. Moving among diverse cultures has taught us that the rules of right and wrong behavior are not universal. What one society treasures as its primary values has no counterpart in another. Even the facial look considered "beautiful" in one country is declared ugly somewhere else. Very few of us actually "see" with our eyes (the landscape, the fashion, the village), instead we pre-judge according to unexamined standards.

To see everything in the present requires constant renewal, constant work. It is easy to sit at home bombarded with polluted judgments and prejudices about people and events in foreign lands. When I'm traveling, I'm overwhelmed with the reality of what is actually happening. Since I'm not fettered with local prejudices nor a victim of local bigotry, it's possible for me to be a helpful influence, not by political activism, but by simply being a citizen of the human race.

Of course inevitably I fail to maintain this open attitude and once again become judgmental. When that happens, the sunny day disappears and the fun evaporates. The existing landscape disappears and is replaced by a sad and barren vision. This especially happens when I'm cooped up and stagnant. Time to hit the road again!

A Horrible-Great Sailboat Adventure

After working on our eighty year old sailboat, we took a few trial sails followed by a long passage. During that passage a fierce Mediterranean howler blew out of nowhere. Without warning wind moved from gentle breeze to howling "Force 9," baby ripples erupted into raging killer waves.

Nearly everything on the old boat had been rebuilt or replaced, and she stood out proud and "Bristol Bright." The only things she didn't have were a new engine and replacements for the elderly sails. In that storm, the ropes tore through the canvas and the sails streamed out in tatters like ragged flags. At the height of the storm the engine refused to start. The boat drifted for three days while we worked the hand pumps. Finally, a tanker ship with Captain Good Samaritan in charge towed our boat to Barcelona Port.

We were bone tired and frightened. A few days lapsed before our knees stopped shaking and our spirits rose. It gradually dawned on us that the old boat was truly sound. She had proved her seaworthiness in a fierce trial.

Ashore, we recuperated. Was there real determination to go on? Was this to be the end of a fine fat dream or would we try again? Maybe that storm had been providential: occurring at the outset to challenge an old life pattern.

In the boat yard, generous people—fishermen and the Port Captain—lightened our burdens. We had been rescued from seeming disaster by miraculous events and wonderful people. With such encouragement we kept on going and gained a new way of life, a new inner spirit.

CAMPING FREE

The Way To Go

Free-camping is the true Gypsy way, stopping in the woods, beside a stream, on the seashore, or in a field or village green. We manage to leave campgrounds behind us so as to stay close to nature and closer to the people whose country we are visiting.

If you free-camp you do not need to have a specific destination in mind, nor a campground to reach before dark. This way you can amble along, unhurried and open to many choices of destination. Indeed, free-camping encourages a style of travel that lets you savor each moment: no time imperatives drive you forward, and nothing holds you back. When the mood strikes to stop, you stop. When you chance on a special spot you can linger for as long as you wish: an extra day, a week, a season.

Camping Without Campgrounds

Camping-free is the primary mode when Gypsying by van. Without campground boundaries we are more likely to contact native people and native customs. Without a designated campground, the potential for adventure multiplies. We were astounded at the number of free-campers we met on the way. We found an elderly philosophical couple parked at the edge of a sea cliff, meditating on its vastness. At another time we found a woman camping alone at interesting, scenic ruins busily sketching and painting. And in a wide river bottom under some trees we met a large family camping where they could swim, sun and fish.

We were hesitant about camping anywhere except in designated campgrounds, until we met an English couple traveling in Spain. Over the inevitable cup of tea, they began to recount great places where they had free-camped and told of fascinating adventures that occurred because they weren't bounded by the conventions of a campground.

With their encouragement we tried free-camping, and at once our life shifted into something entirely different. It was evident that formal campgrounds erected social walls while free-camping left maximum potential for broad people-to-people encounters. And unorthodox events erupted where camp site rules didn't exist. Certainly free-camping leaves you more vulnerable to dangers, yet dangers and adventures go hand-in-hand.

Where To Camp

You camp where you wish, using common sense about safety and respect for the landowner's rights. The variety of locations is limited only by your imagination.

Village greens near northern European villages make good camping places. These are public areas for pasturing sheep, and setting up carnivals. Genuine Gypsies often camp here. The town pump is for livestock and campers. Fill your tank.

A churchyard can be safe and convenient for the night. We stayed in one off the Autostrada in central Italy. In the 17th century monastery elderly couples gardened in the cloister yard and used the visitors room as a bar. We asked if we could camp in the large grassy yard. Indeed we were welcome and as soon as we were settled the men invited me to join them for a drink. After a few rounds we sang soldiers songs together in Italian and English. The bawdier words were omitted out of respect for our surroundings.

Castle Grounds

Old castles make exciting campsites. Walking in the moonlit ruins you can imagine life in Medieval time. The soft moonglow lends romance to harsh stone walls. From a castle in southwest Portugal we watched a blood-red sun sink over an ancient battlefield and, in the distance, the blaze struck the tower of another castle astride its hilltop.

City Parks

In cities, a park, deserted at night, serves as a campsite. Winding roads and paths hide secluded areas just right for camping. In Barcelona we have stayed in Parque Montjuich for several nights while we waited for booking on the Balearic Islands Ferry. We were visited by the Guardia Civil who made us feel very secure as they patrolled through the night.

We've stayed in El Retiro park behind the Prado Museum in Madrid and so were right in position to enter the gallery first thing in the morning.

Gravesites

So many large graveyards lie across older, man-made landscapes that they are especially well suited for the living as free campsites. We have joined with the message on the headstones in expressing heartfelt thanks for the quiet peace there. Due to the townspeople's fear of spooks, or something, travelers are left undisturbed along with the permanent residents.

Alhambra Free-Camping

Our favorite Spanish park lies beside the gardens of the Alhambra Palace in Granada, Spain. We free-camp there frequently while leisurely exploring the restored Moorish palace.

We had read about it as children, had grown up with drawings of its courtyards and towers and expected to see a fairy-tale palace in an alluring setting. We expected something wonderful and yet what we actually walked into was far beyond our most exaggerated dreams. It looks as if a genie has pulled the Sierra Nevada mountains from the sea, crowned them with forests of pine and chestnut and topped them with snow-fields specifically as a setting for this magnificent palace. It is hard to conceive of mere human beings designing and erecting the Alhambra. A great Magus commanding an army of giants and gnomes, fairies and elves would be more likely; the final decorations set in place by sprites.

We push through rings of guarding walls to gain access to a small entrance court where, down a few steps, a pair of wooden doors, ornate with inlaid panels, opens into the audience chamber resplendent with carved and gilded decorations designed to impress visiting dignitaries who have traveled from afar to seek concessions from the Caliph. A balcony hovers at the far end. Were there musicians seated up there? Were there scribes taking down all the incriminating evidence or spies peering down on the men they would condemn? This first chamber is only the tip concealing the Byzantine lavishness of the greater part.

At the rear of the Chamber, guarded doors lead to a glorious sun-filled courtyard. Along the north and south, two-story wings frame the sunny space with its long reflecting pool. All the upper windows are screened with finely turned wood grilles behind which the women of the harem hid. At the west end, a chamber opens off this courtyard. The square chamber, entered through extremely high doors, is typical of all the rooms of the palace with its rich decoration: multi-patterned terra cotta tile floors, a wainscot of genuine amber, blue, green and white tiles cut and fitted into mosaics of intricate geometry, domed ceilings incised in plaster detailing reminiscent of multi-chromed stalactites. The outer windows look up to sweeping views of the mountains and down to the silver snake of the river.

We stop for the delight of this quiet courtyard, these soft dust-colored walls, the bright water mirror, the mysterious grilled windows evoking an ancient and exotic way of life. Empty, uninhabited, with neither furniture, nor rugs, nor accessories, nor any obvious sign of human life, this Palace summons visions of silk robed courtiers wearing elaborate turbans, with servants hurrying to refill bowls of fruits and nuts, with musicians plucking at stringed instruments and dark eyes watching us from behind the grilles.

From Palaces To Parking Lots

As incredible as it might seem, you can even camp right downtown in many European cities. For example, in the parking plaza outside Santa Sophia church in Istanbul you can spend the night for the cost of a small tip to the parking guard. Or in downtown Seville there are large, tree-lined carparks which remain empty at night. Across from them the police barracks watches over you. One can pay for day parking in parking lots and when the attendant goes home, spend the night free.

There is a grand parking lot at the entrance to Venice where wild flowers push up through the gravel and campers invite you to join them for Frisbee or volleyball. You pay a minimum for this vast area set aside for a handful of campers. It was originally built for a thousand tour buses but only about one hundred ever arrive at one time.

We've stayed in parks with lots of cars around us—it seemed that others must be using the park for camping. However, in the middle of the night they turned their headlights on, started their motors and the affectionate "campers" deserted.

Port Camping

Seaports make excellent free-camps since you can use their freight truck parking areas any night. Where waterfront guards patrol the grounds they are secure and safe, and they have the conveniences of all-night cafes and public baths just outside the entrance gates. You'll find other campers near ferryboat docks waiting for their reserved voyage.

Ports are vast stages with high drama. Ships load and discharge exotic cargoes, sailors from far off places swagger ashore, stevedores grunt huge freight loads onto waiting carts. Donkey engines huff freight cars around importantly. Passenger boats depart while people ashore wave frantically to departing friends, as the enormous vessels majestically turn away from the dock. The young crowd ashore catch at streamers flung overboard by friends on the ship while the stewards groan since the streamers flying so gaily are recognizably rolls of the ship's TP. Park and you can sharpen your people watching skills while you watch it all unfold.

Marina Camping

What charms marinas and yacht clubs possess! The camper, who gives himself away by his foreign license plates, is usually welcomed. It is assumed that he is a visitor to one of the boats. Here you can find water taps and all the items of a well-equipped campground, including hot showers and sometimes even electrical connections.

People on boats are eager to strike up acquaintances, share stories, exchange books and invite you to spur-of-the-moment parties. They need your help and your transportation to buy supplies, see a sailmaker, visit a mechanic, or pick up a piece of bulky equipment. This is a chance to maintain the natural, friendly custom of helping other travelers and be richly rewarded with good meals, long talks and the opportunity to learn about boats for sale at super bargains.

Ruins Camping

There are remote ruins where travelers can camp indefinitely. Here there are few distractions. The security guard is a potential friend who may invite you to his home and introduce you to local customs and foods.

Prohibited Free-Camping

Several countries and localities prohibit free-camping. With the need to restrict sprawl and reduce clutter in the beautiful countryside, most of the Brittany Peninsula is posted against camping except in designated areas. However, this causes few problems since every town provides a rustic campsite in a beautiful setting; and also, many farmers are happy to arrange a quiet spot for you in exchange for a few francs.

The latest Greek tourist literature emphasizes that camping outside designated areas is illegal. Most campgrounds are officially closed except during the peak tourist season, but there is plenty of empty space and welcome given by local inhabitants during the off season. The law was enacted to control young foreigners who were littering the beaches, flaunting nudity, introducing drugs and ostentatiously exhibiting what the Greeks consider shameful sexuality. When they wish, Greek police can throw the book at unwanted strangers. We've often free-camped in Greece and enjoyed a friendly glass of ouzo with policemen.

Around the Mediterranean, numerous local authorities make up— seemingly on the spot—regulations that limit free-camping. We've learned to get in touch with a local citizen who will either reinterpret the regulations or invite us to use his pasture for a nominal fee. We are here to become acquainted and most villagers welcome this attitude. . .and us.

Turkish Adventures

Turkey presents all sorts of excellent free-camping opportunities. We once crossed the Bosporus by ferryboat and ran

43

south along the Aegean coast. We arrived late in the afternoon at the ruins of Troy after the gates were closed, so we pulled over to a corner of the large parking lot and camped. Our first night at Troy, the furious wind threw rattles of sharp gravel against the sides of the van while we snuggled inside. Great gusts gnashed and seethed with the ghosts of Greek and Trojan men slain so many centuries past. We read Homer's Iliad and burrowed back in time to ready ourselves for the morning. When the sun rose, we stepped out of the van to hear Troy's tumbled stones speak.

Later we free-camped near Pergamon. Following a dirt road past low villages and on into the countryside, we stopped on the edge of a wide, dry stream bed under a covering of chattering sycamore trees. Across the road, hidden from view, stood a farmhouse. As darkness fell, the farmer walked over to our campsite where we had built a small fire. He hesitated, then shuffled forward shyly. From a basket he presented some apples and a jug of cool water, his gifts of welcome.

He looked serious about his business: checking our reactions, determining what manner of strangers we were. Acknowledging custom, we smiled our thanks, added two or three words in Turkish—our only Turkish—and offered him a small packet of loukumi. He grunted politely, accepted the candy as he realized we knew the rules. He disappeared into the dark, and about ten minutes later his three small sons scampered into camp, laughing and chatting. They offered us a basket heaped with tomatoes and peppers. We exclaimed in surprise (as required), then found a can of sardines in the van and handed this over knowing that canned goods—big city stuff—are a great luxury in rural areas. The boys stayed to learn about the van.

When they left it was only about a two minute interval before they returned with their sisters—two beautiful girls dressed in layers of brilliantly colored cloth. The girls poured boiling

45

hot milk, thick with sugar, into our glasses. We gagged and choked on their kind offering and smiled bravely. Just then, the farmer returned leading his smiling, fat wife wrapped in layers of filmy clothing—gaudy oranges, greens and fuchsias, topped with a scarf glittering with gold threads. We invited her inside where a matriarch could sit with dignity. For the duration of the visit we grinned wordlessly to show our pleasure, until our faces ached.

Free-Camping As Venture

This back-of-beyond place with its unexpected meetings typifies the best free-camping site. It is as far away from town and highway as possible. Here we get in touch with people and discover the rare flavor of their country. In encounters with farmers, villagers, lonely policemen on patrol we come to know foreign places beyond their facade. Profound insight would require greater mastery of the language but these free-camp encounters run deeper than campground contacts.

Where can you have such encounters? They seem to arrive unbidden. We drive down country roads watching for reactions from people who stare at us as we pass. If they exhibit friendly curiosity and a welcoming smile, we stop and pursue the encounter. We choose an empty, unclaimed spot that poses no territorial threat. That is, we don't get near a farmer's ripening fruit nor too close to his home nor stock.

In villages, we shop at the local stores so people can check us out. Often, an important person strikes up a conversation, or with body language that substitutes for speech, investigates our credentials. If satisfied, he will sponsor us as his prize curiosity.

Your Visit As Exchange

If you are fascinated with the architecture, the dress, the

customs of a strange place, imagine how you must also be a marvel to its people. By encouraging mutual appraisal, exchanging gifts, you open a pathway for communicating and learning.

Free-Camp Necessities

However, free-camping requires a continuous search for potable water supplies and proper places for sewage disposal. You will also want a self-contained electrical power source.

Besides the normal built-in water tank, you must store extra water in jerry cans so as to have enough no matter what the free-camping site offers. We adopted the habit of topping up water supplies whenever we could.

Because there are no dump points, self-contained portable W.C.'s are the recommended equipment in vans overseas. Carry a spade to dig a residue pit.

Either photovoltaic panels or a generator is needed to recharge batteries so that you can prolong your stay. Free-campers equip themselves with easily stowable folding tables and chairs, rugs and cushions so as to transform an ordinary field or woods into a luxuriously furnished outdoor terrace.

Free-Camping Cautions

Free-camping can include danger. There is no fast rule as to what dangers might emerge so be prepared to move on.

One very popular winter free-camping area lies on a sandy beach on the Atlantic coast of Morocco. You can reach this spot by driving on the coast highway twenty miles north of Agadir where you'll see a cluster of at least 100 vans camped from January through March.

Since some young Moroccan men eke out a living preying on foreign tourists either as insistent "guides" or as outright thieves, campers along this beach bunch together. These youths act as if it's their right to pick from tourists much like farmers harvest their crop. Campers put their gear undercover at night and lock their valuables. By taking these few precautions, you can spend months without incident. The site is worth the trouble.

Trouble usually erupts when too many tourists invade areas that were formerly dominated by traditional peasant values. Watch for the signs of trouble: rows of curios shops, ranks of tourist busses and rumbles of young men lounging around doing nothing.

The ability to free-camp allows you to move a short distance away from trouble spots to find other ideal sites that are both safe and charming.

KEEPING HEALTHY

Health Fears

Happy traveling should enhance your sense of well being and good health. The wrong kinds of stress reactions disappear with the right kinds of stimulation. Fellow Gypsies report amazing gains in healthfulness. We often hear: "Haven't had so much as a cold for a couple years." "By golly, I sure don't understand where my arthritis (back pains, ulcers, you-name-it) went since I've lived on the road. And I don't want to know." "This living out of doors, close to nature, certainly brings back my old pizazz. Got ten years younger!"

When we first planned to travel we heard people complain: "I just can't travel anymore. I get sick every time." We started our journeys wary as mice peeking out of their hole. Tourists tend to be careful about everything. They boil drinking water or treat it with iodine, shun a whole list of mouth watering foods, steer clear of unpeeled fruit, salads which haven't been sterilized in chlorine solutions, restaurants not on some approved list. But we found these precautions to be unnecessary.

Health Attitudes

We have followed the advice of maintaining regular routines, plenty of water, plenty of rest, regular exercise, moderate amounts of food at regular times, not over-doing just because we're not at home and have remained disgustingly healthy through years of travel. And with the fresh outlook on life we've gained, our health has vastly improved. We anticipate an increasingly healthy life as we become older.

Venture Into Health Alternatives

A marvelous British doctor, Aubrey T. Westlake, in his book

The Pattern of Health describes age-old, as well as new, paths to health. He started a flood of research and publications making his discoveries readily available. He calls for a state of "wellbeing" ("wellness"), a condition of not just non-illness but a positive condition of wholeness and health that has all but been forgotten in our modern world. What goes for health nowadays, he said, is a poor, sickly avoidance of the more horrible diseases and a continual propping up with drugs. He regards the typical modern condition as one of anxiety, depression and fear.

Among his treatments Dr. Westlake employed the 38 flower remedies developed by Dr. Edward Bach. This system of healing, Dr. Bach says in his book *The Twelve Healers*, "shows that our fears, our cares, our anxieties and such. . .open the path to the invasion of illness." When the mental condition is changed . . ."then the disease, no matter what it is, will leave us." Quite a few travelers use the flower remedies as their principal method of healing. The current return to ancient knowledge and "alternative" methods taught many of us not to scoff at doctors who read our body condition by studying our eyes, nor at herbalists or homeopaths who "Treat the person and not the disease." In Europe, we soon learned that the term "doctor" encompasses a wide range of licensed health professionals.

Sources Of Health Wisdom

Megan and I trained in the Alexander technique which taught us to inhibit habitual physical responses to stimuli, so as to allow nature to restore our body-minds to their rightful freedom of movement, brightness of eye and outlook. We learned to release the neck and head and let the body follow to find its natural positions. This training enabled us to loosen our habitual, destructive responses.

Part of our travel reading, on a dose-by-dose prescription, is the tough *Course in Miracles*. Through it we stopped blaming the body for illness and came to regard that "good old donkey" as a willing servant if left alone and not overloaded with mental garbage. The course has led us to direct each thought and action according to a single intention: that it be peaceful. With a peaceful intention directing, events and decisions take care of themselves. We're learning to observe but not be concerned by outcomes.

We have no argument with orthodox allopathic medical treatment. We depend upon it for assistance, especially for emergency treatment. Who doesn't still check in with a dentist and take vitamins? The successful traveler delights in open-mindedness.

Vaccinations

Check and double-check vaccination requirements before getting them. The World Health Organization and a long list of countries have dropped several inoculation requirements. At the same time, many U.S. tourist guides still go on insisting that you be injected against diseases that are all but eradicated.

There is a growing belief that anxiety over threatening diseases may be seriously harmful, so if the shots quiet those fears maybe you should get them. In recent years, no country in Europe, the Middle East or North Africa requires any shots. Occasionally there is an outbreak in a limited area in which case we either avoid that place for awhile or get inoculated before going there. Outbreaks are widely publicized as soon as they occur.

Beware of swimming in many parts of the Mediterranean especially in the summer. Due to the inadequate handling of sewage all along the coast, summertime usually involves a health alert even in well known resorts. The chief medical officer in Naples had to leave town after he declared the beaches along that coast a serious health hazard. He was proved right, but the merchants were furious.

Ask Your Doctor

Before you start out: consult your physician. Describe your long-range travel plans. Not too long ago physicians prescribed travel as a cure-all for all sorts of chronic disorders.

When we got organized for our first travel fling, we got a complete check-up from our family doctor: head to toe, inside and out. We were in good shape and there was no evidence of diseases or impending collapse. When we asked him for a full, professional list of recommendations and precautions, he held up his hand and said, "Look here, I'll make only a few suggestions. If you want my best advice, just go have a good time. Now tell me, just where do you intend to travel?"

We told him and he marvelled at the prospects. He asked us to drop him a postcard or two. At least that way he'd get some vicarious pleasure from a journey he wouldn't let himself make.

A Professional's Advice

The limited advice given by our doctor turned out to be absolutely correct. Instead of listing things to avoid, instead of discussing horrendous calamities we might encounter, he gave some suggestions:

☐ What did we think about our own health? Were we full of vim and vitality and ready to go? Or did we harbor doubts about our physical condition? He told us to take whatever steps would set our mind at ease; a positive image of our health would go a long way to keep us healthy.

☐ Drink plenty of water.

☐ Establish and maintain regularity in habits—eating, exercising, resting.

☐ Invite some stress but don't overdo it. Travel can be a positive rejuvenator. Travel signals new demands to the body and mind which respond with creative mental and physical transformations.

Water Regularly

"Drink plenty of water." Of all the advice given by physicians who have studied the problems of travel, this piece of common sense is so obvious it doesn't seem worth mentioning. But once you leave your usual surroundings routines do disappear. Activities which maintain a healthy balance, habitual activities, are often neglected in new circumstances. Drinking plenty of water is just the sort of routine no one can afford to drop.

The Drought On Airplanes

The trip overseas by airplane fully demonstrates the problem. You are enclosed in one of the driest atmospheres possible; it's a sealed capsule delivering metered arid air. In it you're lavishly invited to consume quantities of alcohol. You have to beg for plain drinking water.

You ask me, "What about the drinking station?" Have you honestly tried to quench your thirst this way on an airplane? First, the stuff that comes from the water tank of the plane is chemical-horrible. Second, the collapsible, ten-drop capacity cup forces you to stand at the station, trying to get a proper drink with a dozen refills, blocking the narrow aisle to the restrooms, and holding on while the airplane bumps through the sky.

Aloft, thank the stewardess for her kind offer of gin, bourbon and beer. . . . Then ask the big favor of being served a couple of cans of club soda.

Be Prepared

To be certain of enough water on a plane or train carry your own. You'll look like an eccentric refugee clutching paper bags, yet the slight embarrassment is more than offset by continued good health. For the long trip across the Atlan-

53

tic take at least two quarts per person in plastic, throw away bottles. When that gives out, return to the club soda, even though it's loaded with salt.

After landing, don't leave the airport before you've bought a couple of bottles more. Who knows how long it will take to taxi into the city, find a hotel, etc., etc.?

Dry Run

On our first transatlantic flight we hadn't known about the need for extra water. We arrived in Luxembourg with a parched, dazed feeling and headed for the first cafe in the terminal to get a full glass of water. We shouldn't have bothered. The waitress offered coffee, tea and any number of bottled beverages. "Water," in any language, wasn't to be had.

Overseas, water is not served in restaurants. "Water!" you gasp, only to be met with smiles and kindly suggestions of alternatives.

I once ordered a delicious goulash at a famous Belgian cafe. Taking my selection, the pert waitress made a note on her pad and looked up with a query.

"And what kind of beer does Monsieur wish?"

"Beer? Ah, no thank you. How about some water?"

"No beer?" Astonishment. After all this was Belgium. Then she had an idea. "Oh then it's wine you would like."

"No thanks. How about some water."

When I had finished eating a huge plate of fiery goulash and needed something to quench a four-alarmer, here came a small glass of rusty tasting tepid liquid, a flat, medicinal mineral water.

Your Second Foreign Word

Experience has taught us to learn enough of a language to at least say "pleeze" and "water." The natives consider us fugitives from the desert. It must look comical when we gasp: "Water! That stuff that comes through the pipes!" Invariably this cry brings on a horrified look: "Nobody drinks that!"

Tank Up

Since you'll be traveling most of the time in your own self-contained Gypsy wagon, an adequate supply of clean water is no problem. Fit your van or boat with adequately sized tanks. To fill them, we've found good quality drinking water in villages from Spain to Turkey, from Holland to Morocco and never had a day of diarrhea or any other water-borne health problems. The efforts of the World Health Organization have provided this supply of good drinking water.

"Good" means without harmful bacteria but it does not necessarily mean "delicious." The cities of London and Florence and Barcelona provide over-treated water that is all but undrinkable. In Florence we joined in the local custom of filling up jerry cans at a public fountain near the stadium. It lifts pure, delicious water directly from a deep well.

Water Treatment

When we want to fill up at public taps we look for a responsible official and ask if it's potable. With his affirmative answer and if we judge it good tasting, we act on our blatantly unscientific appraisal. In order to come to your own conclusion, you might want to read the U.S. Health Service bulletins. They say to treat most water supplies overseas with purifiers or drink bottled water. Take your choice.

Everyone knows people who have been plagued with frightening cases of dysentery after drinking water in countries such as India and Nepal. You should not dismiss the possible ill effects of polluted water! Carry purifying tablets or a portable water purifier.

Untreated But Successful

We carry a large packet of water treatment pills that to this day we have not yet opened. We discussed our trusting attitude towards water with a biologist doing water research in Africa. We asked him why we didn't suffer from travelers-tummy, while others did. He enquired about our habits of hygiene, learned a bit about our travels and came to the conclusion that our good fortune was just plain, unadulterated good luck.

He added that maybe our slow traveling style, staying in a place for a long time, gave our body time to adjust to different microbes. And perhaps we had gradually built up an immunity to European bugs that gave us the strength to survive attack. He warned us about tropical areas with Bilharziasis (such as Egypt and Central Africa) and the Orient in which our immune systems would not be able to repel exposure to their virulent microbes.

Rough Roughage

Traveling and sitting still for long periods increase the need for additional roughage to keep the body in working order. We carry a quantity of wheat bran with us and replenish our supply at health food stores easily found in most European cities. Of course we eat plenty of raw salads, fresh fruit and cooked vegetables that contain roughage.

Killer Cash

British research suggests there is a greater chance of catching something terrible from handling paper money than from ingesting food or water. Surely the regularly washed, starched and ironed Swiss francs harbor nothing more than the threat to convert to gold. But the grubby Italian lira notes, especially those of smaller denominations, look as if they

harbor creepy-crawlies. Moroccan bills look like lumps of recycled chewing gum. Experienced travelers learn to wash their hands a half dozen times a day. Others insist only disinfectant will eliminate the money problem.

Dairy Do-Nots

Who hasn't been impressed with the threat of disease in untested raw milk and raw milk products? However, wherever you go you'll find pasteurized milk and cheese available. Of course the back-road villages and ports may not bother with such niceties. It is best to carry cheese from sources of known quality. You can pasteurize raw milk by bringing it to just below the boiling point and holding it there for a full 30 minutes.

The European Economic Community (EEC) nations have set minimum standards for food purity and quality. You'll be pleased to find Danish butter, English cheese and French yogurt in a remote trading post. Since the invention of irradiation, so called "long life" milk can be found on grocer's shelves most everywhere. Perfectly pure powdered milk is available everywhere for us older babies.

Vitamin Supplies

If you are vitamin freaks as we are, take a full load of them with you and arrange for refills to be mailed to you. Overseas the strengths available over the counter are much less than U.S. vitamins. We've been assured by druggists in England that vitamins are useless; the low strengths are the good old government's way of preventing silly people from hurting themselves.

You may have to pay an import tax on vitamins that are sent to you. The rules evolve as time goes by. Even adding the whopping 28% tax, mailed vitamins still cost a fraction of the less potent European brands.

Med Magic Herb

Mediterranean people take doses of garlic, not vitamins. The first ingredient listed in their recipes is garlic; other ingredients are incidental. They claim garlic keeps them free of heart trouble. A Florentine friend is one such picture of health and vigor. She takes her daily clove of garlic straight and continues to garden hard in her eighties.

Too Much Sun

Be specially aware that Gypsying puts you in the sun more than you might be accustomed to. This is even more of a problem for boaters. Increase the recommended sun screening number for your skin by a notch. Some sun-lovers have had great success by taking mega-doses of PABA pills as well as using sun-block cream to avoid sunburn. Get professional advice from a dermatologist before you go.

Regularity

We try to maintain, as much as possible, regularity in all our habits. We keep to routines in exercise, rest, eating times, and amounts of food and drink. Irregularity invites trouble. Having your own self-contained living unit makes it much easier to retain familiar schedules.

Don't push on when the body signals exhaustion. Skip the extra hour tramping through a museum or leaping up from a meal to charge into more sightseeing. There will be plenty of time for everything provided you heed your body's needs.

Viva Siestas!

Welcome to the old Mediterranean custom of the GRAND SIESTA. Previously, we thought siestas exemplified Spanish indolence. But no more. Now we admire the Spanish wisdom.

Shops in the lands bordering the Inland Sea close their doors after lunch for two or more hours. We follow etiquette and tuck in for a nap. The siesta changed our whole perspective. Early mornings are now precious and not to be wasted. Extended evenings are opportunities to read and talk. Each day grows longer and our energy expands. It's as if there are two days where there used to be one.

Stretching Sinews

Exercise regularly! Gypsying usually provides an opportunity to enjoy a long daily walk or do yoga asanas to keep old sinews stretched and pliable. Working around a van or boat requires stretching, bending and reaching in new ways. Climbing peaks, trekking into the wildernesses, exploring remote ruins also extend the range of exercise. Becoming physically strong and robust can be a goal in itself. Why not prepare for a really old age, say, 100 or more?

European Doctors

Most of the younger doctors in Europe speak English and some have studied in the States. Northern European Health Plans include the cost of flights from Mediterranean countries back to their more tightly run Scandinavian, German, Dutch and English hospitals. With the proliferation of foreign colonies on the southern coasts, they've established their own clinics and hospitals run by northern European doctors and nurses with very high standards. In countries with state-run health services, private health treatment is generally cheaper than in the U.S. In the big cities, watch out for fancy doctors excited by the prospect of a "reech American." Discuss fees and payment policies before the consultation begins. Carry the list of recommended European doctors available from the International Association for Medical Assistance to Travelers. They also offer 24-hour assistance in locating approved doctors with schedules of established fees.

When Illness Strikes

If an illness lingers, after a short period of local medical treatment, it may be wise to fly home for a thorough checkup with your doctor. This way you can regain your peace of mind before setting out on another adventure.

Dental Despair

Dentists in England can be excellent. Dentists in Spain used to examine and. . . pull the entire mouthful of teeth. We learned to make a quick trip to England when tooth problems arose. Northern Europe has excellent dentists with the latest tools and techniques. Switzerland's the best and most expensive.

Seeing Clearly

Eyeglasses are not a problem unless you have a difficult prescription to fill. You can get new glasses from the old prescription or get a new exam almost anywhere. We don't recommend this in North African countries though. In Morocco we found they had a formula for "one-pair-fits-all."

First Aid

A "medical travel kit" is necessary for emergencies. You may not have time to translate and treat. It's easiest to purchase a professionally prepared one, complete with bandages, salves and the usual complement of first-aid drugs. Kits can be bought all over Europe in drug stores and auto clubs. Add your own individual remedies to them.

Australian Tea Tree Oil, an all-purpose unguent, is popular with travelers who claim that moles, ingrown hairs, corns, bunions, skin problems, eye infections—the sort of things minor surgery or sophisticated surgery takes care of—can be healed slowly with Tea Tree. You may laugh at Doc Mephisto's All-Round Guaranteed Patented Cure-All yet don't scorn its powers until you've tried it. Ask your physician what he thinks about it. Try your local herb shop for a sample.

Greek Hospitality

On small Greek islands hospitals expect the patient's family to furnish daily services such as meals, laundry, and cleaning around the ward. When a young Cockney friend staying on "our" island had to go in for treatment, we all took fitful turns helping.

He had originally gone to the hospital for a tetanus shot and had been accidentally injected with a horse-doctor's needle full of cholera vaccine! He developed a high fever complicated with hepatitis and was ordered to observation and bed rest.

After a few days, the generous family of the patient adjacent to his bed rescued him from us by taking over the ministrations. Obviously none of us foreigners understood the Greek style of lavish care.

When he was ready to be discharged we had a hard time getting him to leave. He glowed with the clucking attention. Such dolmata, such fine black olives, such a beautiful Greek girl to fuss over him!

The next day he sat dejectedly at a Kafenion, swilling ouzo. To our question of "what's wrong," he replied: "In the hospital I was sick and happy. Here I am well and miserable."

YOU CAN AFFORD IT

Plan From Scratch

Some people would have to stop working to go gypsying. Since their salaries would vanish, they can't see how journeying is possible financially. Others have retired and live on Social Security, a pension or meager savings. They also want to know how to afford travel living. We know people in both categories who have found Gypsying not only possible, but downright imperative after they discover:

☐ Alternative sources for income

☐ How to reduce "fixed" outgo at home

☐ How reasonable initial and continuing travel costs can be

☐ How a small retirement income can be parlayed into almost continual journeying

☐ That a nest-egg can buy many months of travel instead of a few weeks of tourism.

Save Up For Gypsying

Cut down on at-home expenses to provide the wherewithal that gets you going. Sell or lease your automobile. The annual cost of owning and operating a car translates marvelously into round trip tickets. Even if you just put it in storage, the insurance premium drops to a pittance and maintenance all but disappears.

Stop The Outgo

Look at your present monthly outgo. Treat "fixed costs" as your worst enemy. All those things that have meters on them must go! It's time to turn them off. Rent or mortgages, property taxes and insurance, maintenance costs function just like "meters." Cut them in order to be able to start traveling.

Return or sell appliances that a traveler wouldn't require. A Garage Sale can be your Going Away Raffle. When Big Business wants to slim down, it eliminates every possible "fixed" cost including the cost of borrowing. You can do the same.

Start The Inflow

Start those meters ticking FOR you. Lease your house or apartment and let the tenant pay the utilities. Use the income to pay for taxes, mortgage, insurance, maintenance. Store your furniture or rent your house furnished. If you haven't sold it, rent your car to the tenants.

You may already have meters ticking in your favor: annuity, pension or Social Security checks may be arriving regularly. If they barely cover your cost-of-living at home they may support your living abroad in comparative luxury. Some people try Gypsying and find it's ideal for them. They return to the States and sell all their assets including their home. They invest the proceeds and use the income to support travel. Others live on dividends from savings or withdraw the savings as a lump and live on that as long as it lasts.

Investigate possible long distance employment. The company you presently work for may require in-depth reports or reviews of records that can be done away from the office. With computer connections, it's possible to garner income in even remote places. Your particular expertise could be employable although at a slower pace and shortened hours.

Make The Most Of Style

"What will it cost us to go to Europe, to acquire a camping van or boat and start traveling?" That's almost the first question people ask. They're intrigued with the idea, but they're afraid they can't afford it.

When we answer, "It's as cheap as staying at home," they

find that hard to believe. When we revise that by saying, "Actually, traveling's cheaper," they're amazed and ask for details. Indeed it is possible to live very well in most countries on a budget that's at or below the U.S. poverty level. We're talking about having great adventures, eating delicious foods, meeting wonderful people and living without financial strain. However, we caution, how much YOUR particular wandering will cost depends very much on you and how you choose to travel.

To start to project a budget, ask yourself: "What level of expectations do I have?" It is all a question of how you see yourself living and enjoying life. We cannot provide you with figures because actual costs will depend upon the style of traveling and living that you choose.

So ask yourself: "What is my present style? If my usual style costs a great deal, am I willing to change so that I can travel on a long-term basis? What would I expect to get in return?"

Affording it requires some people to adopt a lifestyle where they pare monthly outgo to a minimum. When you're traveling it's so simple: no house payments, no utilities, no car costs, and fewer clothing and food costs. Such a lifestyle is easier to assume away from home because social pressures to spend and keep up disappear.

Style Determines Cost

At the time we started our first adventure, our close friends started theirs. But what a difference. They went as high-style tourists; we went as frugal wanderers. Our friends toured for only a month in France and spent more than we did in a full year. They were moving constantly: first a whirlwind fling in Paris, then motoring down the Loire Valley luxuriating at fashionable hotels, gorging on gourmet cooking and enjoying a busy night life.

We stayed on a small island. We hiked back roads, explored

ruins, learned a little Greek, lived in a rough farmhouse, cooked our own simple meals and spent evenings reading, talking and visiting with other travelers and Greeks.

The difference in cost between the two ventures depended upon location as well as style. They chose France, which was very expensive. We chose Greece, which was not.

Attitude Is Everything

The right attitude is the key to inexpensive travel. Since this is a whole new lifestyle, not a limited vacation, searching for bargains, for example, ceases to be pinching and scraping, and becomes a playful challenge. And the searching itself uncovers more adventures. A friend summed it up: "The less it costs, the more it might be worth!"

Live As A Prince, Pay As A Pauper

In Europe a traveler can go modestly without inviting disease or crime or even discomfort. The choice is not between elegance and sickening grubbiness. No matter what class of hotel, European accommodations maintain a high standard of cleanliness. The price is based on number of rooms, size, baths and so forth.

The same goes for restaurants; low cost is not associated with filth. In Europe you pay dearly for famous names and snob appeal. In modest places the price for good food is the cost for ingredients plus rent and services. Places specializing in hearty meals for laborers produce quality without charging high prices. Less meat, no table cloths, two instead of six courses and fewer menu choices characterize these places.

Most European, Middle Eastern and some North African businessmen habitually eat one meal a day in a restaurant: you should search for their hangouts. Always crowded, always seating the same repeat customers, they exude an atmosphere of camaraderie. The waiters and customers form long-standing friendships and the food warrants returning daily.

In the southern Spanish town of Motril, there is a pension with a restaurant where construction workers regularly eat their noon meal. If you wave aside the proffered expensive menu of "bifstek" and order the "menu del dia," heads will turn, smiles will welcome you, and before long a full litre bottle of house wine will be brought to your table with a loaf of freshly baked bread. Soon a plate of olives and bottles of pickled peppers will appear. The main course comes, perhaps, as potato casserole with blood sausage.

Stick to the daily special and anticipate family style servings big enough for manual laborers, delicious enough to write home about and cheap enough to keep you traveling a long, long time.

A Princely Reward

After a short time spent seeking out the low-cost alternatives, we realized that we were developing a new openness toward people we met in rustic circumstances, at the end of the roughest roads and on the most distant islands. Now we eagerly look forward to this warm human connection everywhere.

Like us, you may climb over a wall that previously isolated you from all foreign experiences and discover, on the other side, people like yourself or reminiscent of your ancestors. Once this happy connection is made, it becomes simpler and simpler to be at home anywhere. If this happens, you will find that your style has changed. And so have you.

Expectations

It's up to you to choose a style and therefore set costs. Ask yourself, what's the nicest way to spend a day? What makes you comfortable? What is fun for you?

Have you traveled to advertized places and encountered jet-set tourists and wealthy natives? Did those people put you at ease? Was it important that the staff spoke English, that the service was first class and the people around you had a familiar look?

Would a small pension on a back street seem as welcome? You'd bump into foreign students and less affluent, native residents. The manager would probably not speak English. There would be almost no service and you'd have to do everything for yourself or with the help of other guests. On top of this, it would be jumping with youthful exuberance: guitars twanging, students arguing and partying. Sound awful? That's what we thought until we tried it. We found such places a challenge and realized challenge was what we needed. We had to learn enough of the languages to make ourselves understood and that made us ready to explore the rest of the country. Meeting local people gave us insight into their culture and ours. Coping with young people forced us to open up, expand our concepts, learn to sing again, and to talk openly about important personal and political matters. Our own youthful fires were rekindled!

The Lean Life, The Fun Life

To afford this life pare down initial travel costs, slim the outfitting and decide to try a modest way. A low budget can lead to creative confrontations and curious confabulations that might not otherwise occur.

Financial strictures lead you to local activities. Would a Greek widow ask a wealthy tourist to help her pick olives? Better believe that is hard work. It led us to an ancient olive press, a mule straining to turn the huge stone inside a 17th century building left by the Turks. This afternoon's adventure led to. . . an invitation to join the traditional life on a Greek island.

If you take an expensive three week Greek tour with guides, visits to twenty islands and thirty temples zapping from bus to hotel to bus, you can lose impressions as quickly as they come. When you live in Greece for a full year on a tight budget your impressions become permanent memories.

Choices And Budgets

In villages and farm areas, the cost of living was so small we found our journey could continue on a monthly outgo of about one fourth the cost of living in the States.

When we wanted to visit cities, go to museums, check into libraries and enjoy concerts our costs rose to about the same level of living at home. Yet by basing our travels in rural surroundings, the savings allowed us occasional luxurious forays into the bright lights we sometimes craved.

Even if you are primarily interested in cities, you can maintain a reasonable budget. Once you have acquired a van or a boat you avoid the cost of hotels and restaurants.

We have explored Rome on two occasions and each time we stayed at shaded and grassy campgrounds on the outskirts and took convenient express buses into the center of the city. Our budget suffered hardly at all. We've stayed in the heart of other cities in campgrounds in Casablanca and Florence, in almost empty parking lots in Venice and Seville, in parks inside Barcelona and Madrid.

The Reasonable Budget

Rule Number One: in order to live within a reasonable budget STAY OUT OF TOURIST ZONES. In The Zone, you will be tempted by a modest looking hotel with rounded marble balconies bulging from her ample bosom. The place looks worn and reasonably priced. Don't be fooled. The room rate could be astronomical!

And right here is a good spot to deliver Rule Number Two: Don't hesitate to ASK FOR RATES, PRICES AND CHARGES IN ADVANCE. Make this part of your new style whether it's a cafe, hotel, campground or marina. If you don't, you will be wide open to embarrassing predicaments. It's all too easy to pay the colossal bill or take the high-priced room in order to avoid arguments.

To avoid this trap we follow the suggestions in guidebooks [See Appendix I] for the moderate-to-low-cost travelers and go to the districts most frequented by local travelers. We wander through tourist districts only as window shoppers. We scrutinize the menus posted outside restaurants. We've learned to smile politely and ASK for prices in advance of ordering any service. Embarrassment arises when you're stuck and it's hard to back out. Check out the situation first.

Affordable Transportation

A simple van enables you to travel cheaply, live comfortably though simply, free-camp and stop whenever you're ready. It enables you to drive right into tiny, fascinating villages, get good fuel mileage and extend your travel with the savings.

A large motor home limits these choices while giving greater luxury, more storage, cooking and living space at a higher price.

Or if afloat, the choice is between boater and yachtsman. A boater anchors in quiet harbors, sails unglamorous waters and heads for fishermen ports. His craft is merely a home and transportation. A yachtsman uses yacht clubs and marinas, and often races competitively. He needs expensive equipment. His craft gives him immediate status, and, for that, of course, he pays.

Food Costs

By itemizing your present food bills and eliminating fancy

items, a basic cost line emerges that is your guide to food costs while traveling. As you travel, exclude foods and other items not readily available; substitute local equivalents and your budget will seldom go higher than at home. This rule won't hold for countries where the farm prices have been kept artificially high such as in France and Scandinavia or those with posh living standards such as Switzerland.

Beef is a luxury in most parts of Europe. The French substitute cheese. In Portugal cheese is not so common nor meat so expensive. In England, lamb is common. English cooks prepare Bedouin, Indian and Irish lamb dishes. In England oranges and lemons are sold singly and expensively. With the Mediterranean almost fished out, one fresh seafood meal will blow your whole week's budget. In Southern Europe, the Middle East and North Africa, local vegetables are available all year.

A tight budget relies on dried staples—beans, peas, rice and cod fish lead the list. How about cod cakes, cod stew or even cod curry? Sounds desperate, but they are surprisingly good. Or that old Greek standby, rovithia—boiled chickpeas poured over rice, topped with fresh chopped onion and toasted sesame seeds. It's delicious.

Stock your traveling home with quantities of grains, seeds and nuts to combine with fruits and vegetables for a complete protein as the Europeans have been doing for centuries. These vegetable-grain combinations are not sorry, tasteless belly-fillers. They are delicious and even addictive.

Experience says: keep it local, buy in season, eat what the natives eat and you will at least stay within your at-home food budget. Or, more likely, below it.

Live Simply

Adopt local techniques, recipes and shops. Traditional societies have faced tough times for centuries and have survived ingeniously. Buy where they buy. Eat where they eat. Live as simply as they do.

The slow, simple, peaceful life can start with the first leg of your trip. You can save money if you travel during seasons when the fares are cheapest. Arrive at your first destination and linger before plunging into the next step. Take it easy, never hurrying to meet a calendar of events. Quiet happiness rather than record-breaking accomplishments guide your travels. Once you've established this unhurried pace, you can pick and choose how much money you spend.

GETTING THERE ECONOMICALLY

The Ticket Tug-Of-War

A travel agent is pulling for a quick sale. You're pulling for economy. For you, saving a hundred dollars can mean a whole extra month of traveling. To an agent it means slouching through stacks of detailed airline or boat company notices. To find your very own travel bargain adopt the guise of a hunter, assume the smoothness of a diplomat. Pounce only when the right price appears.

Here begins your treasure hunt for the BIG bargain travel ticket. Airplane travel is cheapest; boat travel now runs a close second. Super savings are yours for the asking. But you have to ask and ask and ask. Don't use the telephone to communicate with your travel agent. Stalk her in her lair. Don't enter the Agent's cave when she's lean and hungry—busy with the phone, tickling her computer, planning globe-circling excursions for ritzy jet-setters. Go there when she's fat and full—after lunch, in the middle of the week, just as she's breathing slow.

Be a hunter—carry bait. You've come this far in life without a fatal stumble, you know what your personal assets are. Now is the time to use them. Who knows? Thanks to you that agent may become the busiest After-Forty Travel Advisor in town.

The Indispensable Agent

But who said Agent, singular? Why not Agents—plural? One of them should eventually welcome your curious search and offer real assistance. Whatever the circumstances, you need a knowledgeable agent with his notices, his books, his computer to dig up the information that is all but hidden from the public eye. Yet, as is described later, everything is not hidden. Also it is much better to deal with a real live Agent instead of buying your ticket through the mail: if, when about to board, the carrier doesn't accept your ticket or boarding pass, you've got a number to call, a professional individual for an ally.

Know The Rules

Here are hints on how to get the best deals:

☐ Travel in the "low" season which falls somewhere between October and March, varying as it does with each carrier. This applies to airlines only and is a distinct advantage to the Gypsy traveler since he wants to arrive when the slack season gives him more choices in rental equipment, empty campgrounds and uncrowded sites.

☐ Be prepared to buy a ticket from two weeks to three months in advance. This is the period during which APEX (advanced purchase excursion) rules apply or a charter group is being filled.

☐ Be willing to travel "any day" of the week. Often, there are "Monday Bargains" or "Rainy Thursday" excursions. Take advantage of any such nonsense so long as it takes you to where you want to go. This will be a good exercise in the practice of flexibility that you want to develop anyway.

☐ Be alert to the airlines' goal to fill empty seats. The IATA (International Air Transport Agreement) requires that companies sell tickets at agreed, fixed rates. It also includes exceptions—pages of very small print that describe all the ways they can sell below-standard cost tickets. In that small print is your very own personal ticket fare.

☐ Be prepared to accommodate yourself to unusual demands. Your flight may embark at 0200 hours from a secondary airfield 20 miles away. Or, you may be allowed to carry no more than a large purse for luggage, or required to pay for your food. You may be required to accept a destination that is some distance from where you first intended to land, say Brussels instead of Paris. The distances in Europe are short and bus and rail fares are economical, so don't worry about this.

□ Consider a "Stand-by" ticket requiring you be ready to board without reservation. You won't know until an hour before flight time whether there are seats available. Yet this is ameliorated by the nice reservation officers wanting to fill empty seats. Call a week in advance and they'll inform you how full the flights have been and what chances you have of finding a seat.

We flew from Dallas to London and back to the States using standby several times and we never had to check into a hotel to wait over. Stay away from Monday and those periods right after big holidays or the first part of June and September when students are going and coming.

In preparation for getting "bumped" instead of getting aboard carry a lightweight sleeping bag tied to your luggage and stretch out in the lounge for an airport snooze until the next flight. You'd be surprised how many dignified people spend the night at airports snoring unperturbed.

□ Be prepared to join a "Charter" or "Tour Group" who claim kinship to some outrageous belief or esoteric study but welcome all manner of travelers to the flight. For a minute portion of the regular commercial fare, why not rush to join "Liberal Library Learners" or "Friends of Italy?" Ask around. Good bets are service clubs, church societies and ethnic clubs. They may want you badly if their minimum quota has not been filled. We traveled from Denver to Frankfurt in a large group on a Lufthansa Jet with marvelous service and excellent flight equipment. In flight we wondered how had all these joyful people around us had become — "Serious Students of Stained Glass?"

□ Expect to pay 50% less than a Tourist Class ticket!

□ Know that bargains exist in one-way fares. Every airline

has a handful of one-way seats to sell.

☐ When a new route is inaugurated, most airlines start with a 30-day super-dooper savings ticket. Agents have advanced notice of these. Ask. Ask. Ask.

Bargain Bucket Shops

In addition to your travel agent, go to a big-city "bucket-shop" offering fantastic savings. With a planeload of empty seats facing an airline, a sales executive unloads a block of seats to one of these wholesale operations. This block of seats is treated as a charter group. Pick up a Sunday edition of any big city newspaper to find little boxed ads offering: "CHEAPEST FARES to Anywhere/Call Mabel at. . . ." Getting one of those tickets may involve making an appointment, going to some strange address and knocking at an unmarked door.

A British Gypsy needed a ticket from London to Mallorca and found just such a teasing ad in the London Daily Telegraph. He made the appointment and headed for the address given. At the unmarked door, wailing Hindu music oozed from cracks around the edges. He knocked and the door opened a crack. The smell of spiced curry wafted out. A woman, heavily veiled, peered from the crack. Wrapped among the folds of her silk sari was a baby busily nursing.

"Sorry," he managed to gasp, "Er, . . . must have the wrong address."

"You want teeket?" snarled the woman's voice from beneath the veil.

"Why, ah, . . . yes." Not sure he still did.

She faced inward. "Gee-orge, Gee-orge!" she screamed, then shifted into Hindi or Urdu or something, dropping her husband's alias. Standing outside this ill-fitting, garishly painted door in a London slum, it finally dawned that he ought to be asking himself questions, especially, what on earth was he doing there? Just before sprinting off, "George" arrived and shouldered the woman aside. Sullen, unshaven George scratched his sleep-swollen face, belched, turned around, and motioned for his customer to follow.

Our intrepid Brit, having gone this far, wondered: "What would 007 do? Would 007 pass through that door totally unarmed? Wouldn't he carry a deadly sleeve dagger, a fast-shooting Beretta tucked in his waistband and a blood-honed blade in his hollow shoe heel?"

Inside, drawn shades left little light. George collapsed behind a desk in a broken chair and looked up with the dirtiest yellow eyes this side of a mangy cat. Thrusting a hand forward, rubbing thumb and forefinger together he whined, "The moneeey. . . ." He sounded like Peter Lorre.

The British gentleman flew on a top airline with excellent service and no reference was made to his low-low cost ticket while he enjoyed two glorious weeks sailing out of Andraix, Mallorca.

You don't have to go lurking in back alleys. You can find nice, clean, businesslike bucket shops on main streets prominently displaying travel posters like full fare agents. Many travelers use them regularly. Expect all kinds of bargains from 25% to 70% below conventional Tourist Class fares.

Check with travelers who have used them. It's important to get a receipt for your money, a bona fide ticket and, if possible, a boarding pass. Some places can only give you an interim ticket to be replaced with the real thing a day or two later.

It's not a good idea to accept only the receipt that some buckets shops offer. The receipt is supposed to be exchanged for a regular ticket at the designated airlines counter on the day of the flight. Most such offhand papers are legitimate, yet individual ticket agents don't always know their supervisor has sanctioned them.

A good example of major bucket shop advertising can be found in a copy of the twice-a-year special Sunday Travel Sec-

tion published by the New York Times. Usually in Spring and Fall they issue colossal editions on the latest travel news. To the back, in the ad section, there's a chance to compare prices among the bargain basement ads.

Travel Section ads often offer round-trip flights, including three nights in a hotel and all meals, for a fraction of a conventional one-way ticket alone. If you buy the package and don't even use the return, you're still getting a substantial bargain. Better yet try to sell the return portion when you arrive at your destination.

Group Fares

Check with a young relative in college or college bulletin boards to find what charter flights are being offered to students. Often priced ridiculously low, they're worth trying to meet "student" qualifications which may be pretty loose or even allow for "accompanying tour leaders." By this they mean: whoever has the brass to step up and fill the plane.

Through Fares

Living in the middle of the States used to present a cost problem since the fare to a port city was equal to the transatlantic cost. Now several inland cities such as Denver, Chicago, Dallas, St. Louis are starting points for international travel, where you can take off directly for London or Paris and beyond. The direct-flight price beats any combination of domestic-plus-overseas tickets.

The Military Connection

For retired Service personnel Military transport provides an unparalleled bargain. A well-kept secret, properly qualified Gypsies can take standby flights to Europe and the Far East for the cost of a case of beer.

Avoid The Round Trip Trap

Unless you are planning a short trial at Gypsying, you'd be better off without the threat of a cut-off date. Usually the maximum limit of stay is one year. For many of the cheaper airline excursion tickets the limit is even shorter, often six weeks.

Checking Credentials

Bargain tickets can sometimes be bought from a passenger who has cancelled his travel plans. As with the round-trip half ticket, you travel on a ticket issued to someone else. This may work fine. Or it may not. Once in a while, an airline (or a country supporting its subsidized airline) gets sticky, foolishly insisting that your ticket and your passport carry the same name. If you are blond, snub-nosed, freckle faced and female, blandly stepping up to present a ticket that has written in block capitals "Mr. Allibaba Ibrahim Raasheid" may cause you problems. Many agents nod and tear off the ticket and hand you a boarding pass. Others, clearing the throat, fix you with a steely gaze and thrust out a paw: "Your passssssport!"

To avoid the problem of paying for a ticket that possibly you can't use, meet the seller at the airport for the exchange. Borrow the ticket, take it to the counter and show it to the agent to see if he'll give you a boarding pass. If he will, complete the ticket purchase.

Short Term Bargains

An option for the part-time Gypsy is to purchase a six-week, all-inclusive ticket that takes you to Europe and back. It includes a fully furnished apartment and ground transportation to the door. These bargains are winter excursions advertised in the northern U.S.

Alternatives Always

If you hear that all the scheduled airlines have eliminated cheap fares don't panic, go on looking. There always will be alternatives. Enterprising entrepreneurs find ways to skirt around the international airline agreements to offer cutthroat competition. Our first economical journey began with Icelandic Airlines which still flew propeller driven aircraft when all the other lines flew jets. We returned a year later on an even cheaper ticket on the most up-to-date airline in the world. We booked it through a Greek agency. Its jet aircraft shined with newness, its food was the best, and its smartly dressed stewards hovered with deluxe service. And yet it wasn't scheduled, had no executive or ticket offices, and even its name was unknown to most travel agents. With one of the largest fleets in the world, you'd think its owners would advertise. But Congress DID learn the name and its CIA ownership and demanded it be shut down.

Many large airlines appear to employ its planes—same name on fuselage, same crews, same departure gates—on cheapy-charter flights. We once bought a "Viking" ticket and boarded a KLM plane. Iberia competes with itself under two other names and other airlines do likewise. Bucket shops mysteriously manuever to find these bargains.

By Ship

Crossing the Atlantic by ship is more expensive than flying. Of course, if airfares again zoom skyward, this may not remain true. The fun of a slow journey by sea with a private cabin, sea air, good meals, deck chairs and time to make a transition full of reflection may be something you cannot resist. If your travel agent can't help you, get a copy of the ABC Shipping Guide and settle back for an intriguing read. There are a few boat fares priced about the same as the airfare. From Montreal the Polish Ocean Line goes to England and Holland. Their passenger ship, the Stephen Batori, will take a camper as cargo. From the East and Gulf Coasts, the West German freighter line Egon Odendorf carries bulk cargo on non-stop trips to Western Europe. Their ships each have two superb passenger cabins. Prepare for about fifteen days at sea. Most of the other passenger-carrying freighters charge three to five times the air fare.

It's Cheaper To Return

It is cheaper to return to the States than to go to Europe; London to New York can be 10%-20% cheaper than New York to London. If you don't find this price difference at the first agency, try someplace else. There is always some mumbo-jumbo about exchange rates to explain it all away, but you can avoid this in London's numerous bucket shops.

A Tale Of London Town

Sauntering down the high street in the Earl's Court area I had no trouble at all finding a brightly postered agency where a card advertised "Cheapest Fare to Anywhere." I already possessed the return-half ticket from London to New York. So as to complete a quick round trip business jaunt, I needed the other half to fly from NY to London.

"Morning. I'd like your quote on the cheapest fare to New York." It was obvious from my breezy manner that I was a sophisticated comparison-shopper.

"Certainly sir. Won't you have a seat?" To see what I knew, he flipped open his book for a glance and proceeded to quote a normal second-class, one-way fare.

"Thanks," I said quickly. I turned and started to walk. What a way to show him the old bazaar-buyers ploy! From the doorway I queried in a bored drawl: "Don't you have something better?" Since he knew that I knew he ran a bucket shop, the hemming and hawing was brief. He "discovered" (here it was) a London-NY special charter fare (surprise) that was much lower.

"That's fine," I said, whipping out my wallet, "Here's the money. Except, how's about writing the ticket FROM New York TO London?" He flushed with a "Why-do-they-always-come-to-me?" look. "You're here but want to get back. . . here?"

"Well, ah. . . I've already got a ticket TO New York, I don't want another, I want a FROM New York one."

"Hm. . .quite a problem you have there."

Three minutes later he sold me a round-trip charter ticket, at a very good one-way price. The London-NY portion was cancelled out.

CURRENCY, BANKING AND INCOME

A Foreign Banking Story

Along central London's streets financial houses stand erectly; the banks' fabled names are barely whispered on tiny brass name plates. We tiptoed into such an awesome precinct to pick up a money transfer from home. Dressed in jeans and a sweater we stepped into the foyer of a private mansion wondering if we were in the bank. We had checked and rechecked the Gresham Street address.

A man in a frock coat silently greeted us with a fractional bow. A butler? After examining our identification, he led us through a door and down half a mile of carpeted hall to a meticulously dressed gentleman seated behind an acre of walnut desk. The banker rose with dignity, beamed a gracious smile and invited us to sit on elaborate Louis-Something chairs upholstered in delicate cream damask.

"Yes," he said, "we've received your transfer." We signed a form. He summoned his secretary, handed her a folder and muttered something under his breath. She nodded and left.

"My secretary will be awhile yet," he said, in the manner of Prince Charles, and added, "I'm afraid there is a bit of a problem."

"Problem?"

"Quite," he replied smoothly. "Right at the moment we don't have any money."

"No money?" I managed to squeak.

"I'm sorry to have to ask you to wait," he replied. "I've sent my secretary around the corner for some."

This was one of the oldest, most respected international banks. It was rumored to have bailed out the Bank of England more than once. All my illusions about London were shattered. Send around the corner? For some money? Like fetching a "cuppa" from the cafe! What kind of Mickey-Mouse operations was this?

85

The bank director seeing our confusion hastened to add: "We,...ah,...don't normally handle it."

Anyone aware of the attitude of the Brits toward money—a filthy commodity—appreciates that it requires some untouchable, some pariah to keep money among his rags and bones and junk. This squeaky-clean institution probably has it fumigated before delivery.

Eventually, in this place that deals in treasuries and in gross national products, we received our few hundred dollars. Looking down at our ordinary, almost scruffy clothes, comparing them to the impeccable attire of the banker and the couturier suit of the secretary, we blushed, grabbed our money and slinked into the street.

Money When Needed

How do you transfer money to another country? How do you order extra money wherever you go? Can you earn money abroad? Let's tackle these questions.

Moving money across national borders is tightly restricted by most countries. The amount you carry out in your pocket, send through the mails or by wire transfers is limited by law. Governments don't want their citizens shuffling currency around without limitations and records. The USA requires you file a report when you bring in or take out more than $10,000 (in the form of cash or other "monetary instruments") on any occasion. Customs officials explain that this has been done to shut down drug dealings, Mafia-style money-laundering and other illegal activities.

Check with U.S. Customs for details about U.S. money restrictions. Consulates and tourist offices provide information for other countries.

Get this information so you can retain legal authority over your money. The problem lies with most governments' misguided assumption that it's THEIR money. At times they want to devalue it and at other times stop its transfer. With the international monetary situation in a muddle, controls on currencies will surely increase. Prepare for this eventuality by placing your nest egg in banks and countries that remain relatively free from restrictions. You are not a crook, and I'm not advising you to do anything illegal. You just want to travel and spend your money where and when you wish.

Traveler's Checks

From the States, take the maximum allowable amount in traveler's checks. Cash can be lost or stolen; traveler's checks can be replaced. Traveler's checks can be designated in the currency you are going to be using or one that you think will stay strong. They can be issued in Japanese yen, German marks, Swiss francs, British pounds and other currencies as well as dollars. While there is no charge for cashing them, there is for changing them into another currency. Some friends of ours bought German marks over a period of a year and found they had increased 25% in value over the dollars paid for them. But beware: the relative value of currencies can move against you as well. Most European businesses prefer Swiss Bankers Traveler's Checks or Thomas Cook's. These can be bought in the States through the American Automobile Association and selected banks.

Beware Of Bank Transfers

Only a few banks in most U.S. cities make money transfers abroad. The rest lack sophistication with the many simple ways it can be done. Consequently, your U.S. banker may employ such complicated ways to transfer money as "letters of credit." What you need is a way to be certain that the money you do transfer will be there when you arrive.

Often money leaves a U.S. bank for transfer to a bank overseas. When the owners of the money go to claim it, the foreign bankers ooze cordiality and helpfulness and cheerfully explain. . . the transfer was not received. It may be months later before the whole thing gets straightened out and the transfer order is "discovered." This is a sour note, not to mention a major inconvenience on which to start travels.

Open A Foreign Bank Account

The best place to start with a money transfer is with a bank headquartered in the country to which you are going to travel. Find a foreign bank—make it YOUR bank! Before going abroad, the simplest way is to open an account in one of their stateside branches. England's Barclays and Lloyds banks have branches in several U.S. cities. Swiss, German and Dutch banks have U.S. branches, too.

Another way is to employ one of the larger U.S. banks that have branches abroad. Open an account, say in Chicago, and make deposits to build up a nest egg for transfer abroad.

Next, have the Chicago branch open another account for you in their London branch (or some other European city) and ask them to transfer the money to that branch; insist on a letter of introduction to one of its officers.

Once you have your overseas account write to your overseas bank officer to tell him you intend to call on him at such-and-such a date. Your letter establishes the contact you need and provides another sample of your signature. The bank officer's reply acknowledges that he knows who you are and that at least some of the money has reached him.

Hard, hard experience has taught many of us: do not trust the efficiency of banks. The biggest and best known can easily foul up your small account. After all, the big banks transfer millions for multinational companies; your measly thousands hardly warm up their computer.

With an account established overseas, you can skip the

bank-transfer path altogether and deposit your money directly. Buy an American Express "Foreign Cheque" through banks that handle their traveler's checks. Just hand over cash, plus a fee, and an Amex agency bank will issue a multi-part check. One goes through their system to arrive at the destined bank; one goes directly by mail; one is handed to you as a receipt. If any one of the systems fail, your copy of the check presented at the overseas bank starts unlocking the money you've sent.

Even simpler, you can often send a personal check on any bank, even a small one, directly to your foreign account. Allow at least 30 days for it to clear. Many of us just deposit a personal check written on our Podunk National Bank account while abroad. It works. Ask your officer at the foreign bank.

A Social Security check is always welcome for deposit and immediate credit.

Your Foreign Banker—Your Friend

European banking is done in the old-fashioned way: your account is handled by one bank officer or his assistant. Your Lloyd's account at the Bedford, England, branch is handled by Mr. Bodkins. You know him—he knows you. When you want to withdraw money at Bedford, ask Bodkins. When you withdraw money in Paris, the Paris branch calls Bodkins.

What a terrific feeling to be dealing with a human being again instead of the unresponsive computer! Your banker becomes your trusted representative. Because of this, it is customary to give that banker your limited power-of-attorney. This way he can withdraw money for you just on a verbal say-so. No check book, no checks. Suppose you have been stuck with unexpected repairs in Greece and don't have enough money. Merely call Bodkins, identify yourself and he will transfer money to a local Greek bank in your name. Just your word does it.

This dealing long distance with your banker depends on personal contact instead of codes, passwords and such. As you talk on the phone, your mind's eye pictures friendly Mr. Bodkin with his sleek grey hair, steel-rimmed spectacles and careful face. He listens and pictures you; you have discovered a common passion for fly fishing and the conversation is bound to touch on that. No matter how bad the phone connection, you will convey with unmistakable syntax or inflection that this is the real you calling. He wants to know if it's sunny where you are (his British city lies under black skies, torrential rain). He hopes that you are having a good time. Another bonus regards money transfers to Third-World countries. Your personal banker will know where potential difficulties lie and ways to get around them. We needed some extra money while traveling in the far Anatolian plains of Turkey and called our Mr. Bodkins. He was horrified at the prospect.

"Don't you know that money gets lost in the banking system there? Hmmmm, hmmmm. But we do have a sort of agent in Istanbul. . . let me see. . . Right, we'll send it today, but be willing to wait for about three weeks. Best we can do. Cheerio."

And three weeks later the money did arrive at a local bank. Where it had 'rested' in the meantime is not known.

There's another personal matter in this super friendly relationship: always carry a balance on the plus side. As a foreigner it is unthinkable for you to write a check for an overdraft. It won't merely bounce, it may destroy a budding friendship.

Banking In Which Country?

Here's a word of caution: CONSIDER THE COUNTRY OF YOUR BANK because some have impossible currency restrictions. And a country's currency may be so weak that your nest egg will be devalued. Mexico is a prime example. A few years ago Mexico's government confiscated dollar accounts.

Your money would have been automatically exchanged for pesos. At the same time the peso started plummeting in value so that in six years a nest egg of $1000 would have shrunk to $25! In some countries you can establish an "external" account designated in dollars. Yet even then, you still don't have complete control. You'd be amazed how much easier the money door swings IN than OUT. Especially if you wish to withdraw cash in dollars. Then the bank takes out a hungry bite as an "exchange fee." Before leaving Greece we wanted to exchange drachmas for dollars. Our local bank was allowed to furnish us only Greek currency. We then had to carry this cash all the way to Athens to the Central Treasury (!), fill out sheaves of forms and wait a day to exchange for much diminished dollars.

Experienced Advice

Don't get caught with money in the bank that you can't withdraw. A few years ago France nationalized its banks and temporarily froze withdrawals. Accounts in dollars could not be liquidated for a time. Transferring any substantial sum out of France is still difficult. This is merely one example of what could happen in a 'modern' yet bankrupt country. Under the English Labor government its citizens could take only 300 pounds sterling out of the country for vacations.

Politicians transfer their economic problems to individuals. You don't want to be a victim. World-wide economic problems are on the rise, but you can still enjoy long-term travel if you know how to sidestep national difficulties. The way recently recommended by monetary specialists is to use only Dutch or Swiss banks. They point out these country's banks have the least governmental interference and their currency is backed by solid assets. One of the world's large banking centers lies in a town in Switzerland a short distance from the Italian border. Why not imitate the canny Italians?

To avoid devaluations keep your account in what's called a "hard currency." Swiss francs are 'hard' because they are exchangeable for gold. Exchange rates, if they even exist for 'soft' currencies are set arbitrarily by the government. Moroccan dirhams, Russian rubles and Israeli sheckels are a case in point. Unfortunately many formerly solid currencies are turning soft, so research the situation before committing your money.

In money matters, change is rapid; good banks turn sour, solid countries fail. Experience taught us to keep abreast of developments and be prepared to shift currencies, banks and countries. You can get advice about foreign banking in books dealing with the uncertainty of the future. [See Appendix B]

Extra Bank Services

Once you have established personal contact with a friendly banker in a country with few monetary restrictions, opened an account, and exchanged your money for gold-backed (politician-proof) currency, you are prepared to travel.

While you are Gypsying, your bank account can be earning its keep. Along with handling money, most foreign banks deal in stocks, bonds and commodities. They will buy and sell at your order or manage a portfolio of your investments. We know a traveling Irishman who makes a handsome living buying securities low and selling high; but to us his success is a mystery.

Your aunt Matilda wants to send you some money (bless her soul). Your foreign bank handles the details while you tour Tunisian deserts.

You want to sell your van or boat. Again, your bank can handle transfer of title and funds while you may be on a trek and unreachable.

When you buy a van or boat in a country with soft currency the seller may be eager to get some of your hard currency.

Strike a deal in his currency. Follow this with a lower offer priced in your own currency and you may find he willingly accepts. You may even be asked to pay to the order of some third, unknown name so that the transaction goes unrecorded. Your bank will arrange the details and advise you of applicable regulations and risks.

Figuring Out Funny Money

The day you arrive on foreign shores your budget is challenged. Here's where you begin to deal in "funny money" — funny because its value doesn't make sense for awhile. You buy a cup of coffee and pay in British pence thinking it cheap, only to discover you've shelled out the same or more than you did at home. Remember you exchanged more than one penny for a pence. You start to pay for that Italian "cuppa" and your bill calls for hundreds of lira. "Wait!" you shout. But the cost may be only a few pennies. You're ready to agree when you overhear travelers who have visited seven countries in five days groan: "Why can't they just use dollars?"

It's a truism among travelers that the first day spent with a new currency blows a week's budget. It takes practice, especially during the first days in a new country, to gain familiarity with the exchange rate. This travelers' muddle has been carefully exploited for centuries at ports of entry: astronomical cab fares, demands for whopping tips and lures into hotels built and priced for royalty.

Travelers' Muddle Resolved

The best treatment for "travelers' muddle" is simply to stop immediately upon crossing a border. Find a quiet place to rest for a few hours or days.

Test the currency by buying a familiar item like a bottle of milk or a loaf of bread. "You mean it takes two thousand lira

94

to pay for that milk!" Lay out a sum of the new currency in an amount that equals one dollar. What could you buy for that dollar at home? What will that amount buy in this place?

Look forward to the day when you can lay out that dollar equivalent and receive twice or three times what you expected. The right response to that is an immediate "Let's stay."

Going carefully and cautiously the first day of handling a new currency is the first step to going cheaply. Next, acquire a sense of the relative prices in the marketplace. After using honey for sweetening at home you might think nothing of buying a pound jar (a half kilo) in Greece only to find that sweetening with liquid silver would have been cheaper. Honey is an expensive delicacy in Greece while rich, full-bodied retsina wine that would cost a bundle in the States is cheap.

Earning Money In A Foreign Country

We have yet to find a country that allows foreigners (yes, you are a foreigner abroad) to sell or charge for labor or services without a work permit. For the most part only movie stars rate them. A few years ago, the British used to make a point of this by stamping your entry visa with "work not allowed." Don't count on earning your basic maintenance abroad.

Supposing you can get away with it, will the jobs be available? Traveling to places where the cost of living is lowest puts you smack in the middle of an economy of the unemployed. If a foreigner were to earn money there he would compete with unemployed citizens. When you travel to a country where the cost of living is high you'd be contending with very young, very bright, multilingual, highly trained people. You might sweep floors there.

Work Is Just Possible

With that said, some travelers have earned money to help

fill out their meager finances. In the wine regions of France, especially around Bordeaux, you can earn room and board and some money during the grape picking season. Vineyards need all the extra hands they can get and many Frenchmen feel it beneath their dignity to do this manual work.

In November in the Peloponnesus of Northern Greece the citrus crop ripens into another picking season. Living conditions are cruder than in France, and you must dicker over your wages, but the proceeds enable you to extend your travel.

Artists and craftsmen have the least difficulty finding income opportunities. Foreign sidewalk artists sit alongside local resident artists doing portraits in Florence and Rome. If you look the part there is no hassle: show a shaggy beard, sport a beret, wear paint spattered clothing, look hollow-cheeked and hungry eyed. No one will ask for your work permit. But you have to be very, very talented to compete.

You may be startled to work beside an Italian-looking artist who kids the customer in a thick Italian patois, collects his money after handing over a very handsome portrait and then turns to bum a cigarette from you—speaking in a broad Iowa accent.

You might try the luck of one very special English family earning money in Italy. They perform as clowns, mimes and acrobats who put on a good show in plazas and beside street markets. The police occasionally harass them but they are so funny, so harmless, so attractive that the crowds quickly brush officialdom aside.

A good street musician can ply his trade almost anywhere. An example is a superb violinist from London's Royal Academy of Music who played on the Ponte Vecchio in Florence. His hat, upside down on the pavement, overflowed with bills after a wonderful Bach partita.

A developed talent or profession provides numerous ways to find temporary work. There is a fine doctor who returns to England for a six week stint in the winter to substitute for doctors on holiday. British and Americans tutor spoken English in established private schools or start their own to serve Europeans who wish to perfect an accent. A highly regarded acupuncturist holds special classes with physicians. An English painter ships sunny Spanish landscapes to a London dealer.

A writer can continue his writing or a not-yet professional can break into the market with travel articles, but be aware that some U.S. travel magazines are notorious for either not paying or dragging out the payment for years. Check with professionals who can advise on the legitimate ones. Retired journalists send occasional dispatches from abroad to their former employers such as the American woman who has lived for decades on her income from "Letter from Paris."

Handcrafts such as knitting and crewel work, if distinctive, can be exchanged for produce. Traditional folk respect fine craftsmanship but don't expect cash in their barter economy. Your own patterns and details may start a local craze. But then again there are crafty markets amongst the not-so-traditional: one woman squanders a half-thimble of cotton yarn with each complete crocheted bikini she makes for a Paris shop.

Boat Money

A really good motor or electronics mechanic will be able to work around marinas. A foreigner working for other foreigners lives in a smoke screen on the waterfront. Without any forms to cover such a situation most port authorities don't want to see what's happening. And, there is a quasi-legal status to a boater working on other foreigners' boats. The worker steps from his slice of sovereign territory (his boat) to work aboard another slice of sovereign territory. All very legalistic but more important, not threatening to the locals. A justly famous American shipwright repairs boats abroad with no problems. When he has a large job he hastens to hire local craftsmen at unaccustomed high levels of pay. No complaints are heard. Nor does he stay long in any port.

You can go through the process of signing-on as crew to the boat on which you intend to work. Yet, at any time, rules or not, capricious AUTHORITY can step in to stop you. Those who establish friendly relations with the locals, don't talk about their wages and move elsewhere after a few months seem to escape this authority. Always ask others about their experiences.

Sailor's Work

If you are an experienced sailor, there are opportunities for boat deliveries, or you can earn money crewing on long ocean passages. Several American and English boat delivery specialists headquarter in Mallorca, Spain. It's possible to establish a charter business for guests sailing with you from port to port in the Mediterranean. One enterprising Dutch couple did this in Spain, always returning to the same port. After seven successful years, the police inquired into their permit. They quickly moved to France. Another less lucky Dutch couple ran two successful seasons until their boat was confiscated and sold at a rigged auction to the port captain's brother. The trouble was that their boat was a beamy steel ship with powerful engines that would (and finally did) make a fine fishing boat.

A disarming German fellow has been earning money for years chartering in and out of Spanish ports. His short stays, his ease in dealing with fishermen and officials assures him of welcome wherever he goes. He helps Spanish fishermen paint their boats, splice ropes and mend nets always making himself a good neighbor. He has no problems.

WHERE TO FIRST?

The North American Alternative

Although this book describes events abroad, you don't have to go that far for the Gypsy adventure. There are places in North America with fascinating challenges that can change your life.

Challenges are certainly everywhere, even in your own home. But even challenges can become commonplace when their setting remains always the same. Vacations shake up our blunted senses and freshen our dulled lives, but long-term travel in the Gypsying mode offers both refreshment and a whole new life. It requires you to go where your culture, your language and dress are not the norm, where your citizenship and your name appear unusual and your face peculiar. Go where you stand out as THE FOREIGNER; then you'll begin to feel changes take place within yourself. The edges and interior of North America (islands, remote deserts, barely accessible areas in the U.S., Canada and Mexico) offer you the chance to explore, as do enclaves such as Indian reservations and areas where immigrant groups have retained their culture.

Start With Familiarity

Choosing the first stopping place is most important. The right place will awaken your sensitivity gently with little shock. Too much foreignness at the outset could throw you off.

Family Ties Abroad

If you seek adventures abroad and have relatives in "The Old Country," make them your first stop. You could be one of the lucky ones whose mother's first cousin has written to invite you to please come over to renew family ties in Greece! Or grandpa Meier, still the mainstay of the north German clan, would welcome a long, long visit from you just to see what changes have been wrought in the family character after so many generations in the New World. France, Italy, Holland, and other lands call through family voices. Naturally, you go there first.

But if you don't have someone waiting, someone who will make your first days in foreign surroundings uncomplicated and refreshing, then you may want to land on English-speaking soil, stay at an English inn and eat at restaurants with readable menus.

England is a good place to start this new life, make first arrangements, make the first banking contacts and look for transportation.

English Language Barrier

But don't assume that you'll be fully understood in England. We speak Americanese, a rather obscure dialect not deemed sufficiently civilized to warrant careful attention. If you find some guttural pidgin English dialect among African bushmen totally incomprehensible, then you have an idea of an Englishman's attitude towards what we say. Therefore, don't get into any serious negotiations with an Englishman speaking impeccable "Oxbridge" until you've either found an interpreter or taken a course in English-English.

The English rules about words are different. Not totally unlike Americanese, just different. For instance, we both have rules about what's unspeakable. Without knowing exactly what ought not to be said, Americans turn what sounds like an ordinary conversation into a shambles. Take money. Talking aloud about money is considered obscene. One does not, repeat, does not overtly mention money.

England gave us the opportunity to dip a toe into the fantastic experience of foreignness. The English spoken down in Cornwall had added an "r" clutching at each syllable. We had to listen closely to detect meanings; it was hard not to believe it wasn't an unknown tongue. Up in Scotland the "oi's," throaty "hrrr's" and "rurr's" brought to mind a shaggy lion's purr.

Among such ordinary conversations on the streets or in shops, among such inflections, additions and mouth workings you have the unique impression of entering a theater in which you look upon a marvelous foreign world going about its business unmindful of your presence. A shift occurs, you're in the scene but not of it, discovering that this plot will unfold, as unfold it has for centuries, without you contributing anything at all. You have the first intimations of looking, listening, observing yet remaining almost invisible until you feel ready to mingle. Here is the world you will pass through, interacting with it when asking directions or buying food, but where you are free to remain in the audience watching the pageantry.

You may like the disconnection this creates as all that activity "out there" no longer appears so deadly serious; it's rather like walking onto a make-believe movie set. With this discovery, both the world immediately in front of you and the remembered world back home begin to loosen their hold on you. Gentle, happy laughter comes easier.

Communication, Not Just Language

I once went to shop for a second-hand camper. Of course I was looking for a certain quality at a certain price. The salesman nodded sleepily. Then I mentioned money and he turned death-white. I'd mentioned THAT topic. He shook himself and quickly changed the subject.

We toured the lot discussing the features I wanted. We stood beside a likely camper sitting brilliantly shiny and attractive. In those days I still didn't know the English rules so I unabashedly asked the price. He coughed politely, scribbled a hasty note, folded it twice and without a glance thrust it towards me.

He looked off into space whistling a tune like a schoolboy who hoped the teacher wouldn't catch him doing a naughty thing.

The unfolded note revealed a price three times the value of the camper. Mistakenly I opened my North American mouth to politely ask if a lower price might be in order. He lifted his nose, twitched his shoulders and left.

Before approaching another dealer I conferred with an English friend who'd lived in the States. He guffawed. "Don't you know that we think about money whenever we aren't thinking about sex? But neither is mentionable. What you did was absolutely awful. Now here's how you proceed...."

At the next lot I was prepared with my own hidden, folded note. A brisk, self-confident, salesman hastened to assure me that he was entirely at my disposal.

Avoiding the chitchat, I slipped the salesman the note, shuffled off to a corner and pretended not to watch as he opened it. He turned his back, as if adjusting trousers in private, and read.

After a thoughtful pause he took my arm to steer me to one of the vans. "Look, there, absolutely smashing coachwork." (It looked like a standard factory truck to me.) "You will notice the delightful special fittings." (The insides were crammed with plastic junk). "You're lucky to be shown this superb beauty. Confidentially, a member of an... ahem, distinguished family, had it crafted for his personal use." Never a word about the note OR about price.

Next day, I turned to my English friend once more. He laughed about the whole thing, volunteered assistance and in one short afternoon helped us find the perfect van at the right price. And (would you believe?) without once blurting the unmentionable.

Easiest In England

Despite this subtle communication barrier, it's still easier to start out in England than in France, for instance, to find camping equipment and travel information. If you don't speak professor-perfect Parisian French, salesmen won't even look at you. In England, arrangements are simpler. You can understand at least thirty percent of the information you receive over a telephone. England has all sorts of directories and special magazines for second-hand goods that will give you a rough idea of what's available and at what price. "Better" or up-market goods haven't been priced; for these you have to go through the old rigmarole.

However, those who have stayed in England a few months report they learned to communicate pretty well, made deep friendships and even gained the good manners of not mentioning you-know-what.

Our First Adventures In Foreignness

Another reason to begin in England is her historical relationship to the United States. We strolled through villages built of limestone more than 700 years ago whose straw thatch roofs dipped nearly to the ground. Under the thick straw roofs, door lintels were chiseled into fantastic designs constructed somewhere between Leif Ericson's and Columbus's voyages. Small bay windows pushed out at corners with panes of hand-blown glass. In them we often saw fat cats permanently lying in wait for sunshine. Most streets were unpaved, narrow and winding; houses lay against the street protected only by a thin border of brilliant flowers. The very coziness of this concentration contrasted sharply with our tall cities and scattered suburbs.

London

Spending time in London will allow you to enjoy its uniqueness: St. Paul's Cathedral, Trafalgar Square, Oxford Street and more. But even more special are the intimate scenes in

this grand city. The inner City of London tightly crawls along twisting streets. International firms of great renown surround banking houses of stupendous power. In the midst of this, in the clearing of a little square rises the exaggerated steeple of a modest Christopher Wren church, a village parish church. Here and elsewhere we realized that London, one of the largest and most imposing cities in the world, is made up of a cluster of villages where there are so many green parks that wild rabbits can be seen hopping about in the early morning.

The English Experience

One of the primary delights in England is to stay in an old-fashioned Bed & Breakfast. This is a small hotel or converted mansion where you can spend a comfortable night in an heirloom bed, then wake to a full bacon-tomato-baked-beans-and-eggs breakfast served in a flower-filled dining room.

And, when you do buy a camping van, it is not too difficult to engage a top-flight mechanic to go over it and put it in good condition. You'll be able to converse on the technicalities and find parts. You can count on excellent maintenance and advice. Always settle the price for his work in advance IN WRITING. Employ your nasty old North American habits or you'll regret it. The taboo about money-talk can be used to hide deliberate overcharges.

The English experience delivers minuses as well as pluses. Their frightening driving speeds along with their rule of driving on the left side of the road can make you wonder why you came. After a lifetime of driving on the right (with steering wheel on the left of the vehicle) your left-hand attempts may land you in a ditch or find you lurching up on sidewalks in attempts to escape the mad Englishmen coming from the other direction. You come to a major crossroads, glance the wrong way, flick back to shudder at the traffic about to clobber you and your brain blows a fuse.

England For Information

England is carpeted with English-speaking consulates and tourist bureaus. They offer foreign guidebooks for free that you would have to pay for in the country where they are printed. Visas, costs, sightseeing and customs regulations can be discussed in London before you ever go to the continent.

England For Boat Buys

In England, you'll probably be able to find a good boat, and professional quality boat yards to help with outfitting, repair and maintenance work that a second-hand boat will require.

There are plenty of experienced sailors in that seafaring nation where a large percentage of people own their own boats. You'll even find mariners who can be hired to crew your craft. Since you may wish to poke into some charming English harbors and estuaries, they can teach you the tricks of navigating in English waters and avoid the perils of overfalls, sand banks and tidal races that move faster than your sails or motor can resist.

England is famous for its sailing schools. You can learn from scratch or improve your existing sailing skills. Either way you'll gain the confidence that will set you on your way to becoming a fine old salt.

England For Jetlag Recuperation

England is also a good place to hole up for a few days and recover from jetlag. Those who press on unmindful that their inner clocks lag behind the swiftly moving body soon tire, blaming the venturing itself instead of marking it down as a temporary condition. England offers plenty of quiet places to wander each day without undue stimulation. A few days of this sort of rest get you ready to make further plans. You can now think about climbing the snowy Jungfrau or braving the hot and sandy bazaar at Timbuctoo.

Last Stop For The Almost-Familiar

England is your half-way staging post, familiar as well as unusual. The meals start with familiar ingredients. The roast beef is good or better than you're used to. However, the Yorkshire pudding, the way it's made in Yorkshire, is something fantastic. You find the usual fizzy pilsner beer, but England introduces you to brown ale with no fizz, no bitter taste and an unexpected smoothness. You expect to enter a pub for a quick drink only to find yourself lingering a couple of hours in the homey atmosphere chatting quietly with a new found acquaintance. The brisk pace of city traffic reassures you things are much the same here. And, when you do business in an office the transaction is more leisurely and personal. England provides a chance to gain assurance. . .while still being shaken.

SOMETHING NEW — PORTUGAL

A New Country

Remember the times when you have been awed by your first encounter with an interesting personality? Amazed by a new idea or experience? When you enter a foreign country for the first time be prepared for shock and pleasure, and something entirely new and fascinating. Take our experience in Portugal as an example: we had brushed her flanks on the east, touched her head on the north but had never actually crossed her borders to test her charms. Once we did, her land cast its joyful spell.

Portugal's rolling hills, bare rocky peaks, thickly forested slopes and verdant valleys are unspoiled by tourism. They are rich in ancient stones and history amidst a distinctive culture. Unlike Portugal's touristy southern shores, the northern, central and southeastern parts sparkle with plenty of surprises.

Our First Time

Late in August when grapes were thick on the vines, peaches and pears ripe for picking and country folk bustled about at their jolliest, we entered north-central Portugal. Our route lead from mountains to sea, from north to middle and then out across the southeast border. In the valleys nestled brilliantly whitewashed villages. On the rolling plains flowed waves of golden grain, and on the eastern pastures, below stands of live oaks, grazed clouds of fleecy sheep. As we traveled, the very names of the provinces sounded a roll call of extravagant experiences: Minho, Douro, Beira Litoral, Estremadura, Ribatejo, Alentejo.

Along the way, everything was new: new foods, a new language (sounding like Spanish spoken with a mouth full of rocks), new wines, and new peoples. Most of all, Portugal started us laughing and kept on nudging our funny bone. We felt happy after we crossed the northern border and this persisted wherever we went.

Crossing A Border Into Laughter

The crossing was routine: police checked passports, customs men looked at van insurance papers for numbers and date. One of the border guards sauntered towards the van as if to have a look inside. Contraband? Smuggled passengers? Was this to be an annoying search? Not at all. Instead he stopped some distance off and smiled, saying something like: "Nice rig you have there," and then waved us on into his country. His interested expression revealed he was thinking a camper like that would be swell for his family on vacation. No envy, no he-on-one-side and us-on-the-other kind of encounter; just simple admiration.

Our joy started with a young local couple, who lifted their thumbs along the short road to Chaves. The big grin busting out of the man's energetic face and the swell of his pregnant wife's body urged us to stop and offer them a lift. As they tumbled in the rear door, the wife collapsed and smiled in thanks.

The husband pushed his way forward to perch just behind the driver's seat and began a hurried, noisy conversation as if he had just met up with an old buddy. He couldn't wait to tell us about his walking trip across the Spanish border to buy ham. The meat must have contained some powerful magic to have warranted such a hot and exhausting hike across the border and back.

As we rolled down the road he wanted to know everything. Where were we from? Where were we going? How long would we take? With difficulty, I explained that since I spoke some Spanish I could understand some of his Portuguese. "Well. . ." he seemed to say, "try this for size. . ." and started on a long, excited, rambling monologue spurted at maximum speed.

Keep Driving

The only thing I needed to do was continue driving and nod from time to time. His confidential and raucous voice buzzed with laughter at his own jokes and emphasized his warm desire to make us feel at home. As he talked he sweated with enthusiasm, dripped with eagerness—how well we understood him, what a great country we came from, what a hell of a hot day this was! Continuing, he exploded with last minute shouts to turn here and dart through there. Then he suddenly tugged, almost pulling my arm from my shoulder.

Some For The Road

"Stop the truck! Get out! We'll have some wine!" At the side of the road stood a garage attached to a tall house.

"Hurry!" he urged as if the sky were falling. "Your wife must come too!" he commanded. The four of us got out and passed into the shaded doorway to find ourselves in a country grocery-cum-feedstore-cum-bar. From a cooler the proprietress extracted a bottle of red plonk without waiting for our host to order. Grabbing glasses, she hiked up a corner of her apron and wiped them.

Our host's wife declined with muttered thanks and held her heavy belly. One of her good days this was not.

In the bar, several rustic types sat on barrels, hay bales and rickety chairs. Our host introduced us to all his friends explaining, in some mountain dialect that entirely obliterated the Portuguese; "Look at these people. They are Americans! They have done us a service," and on and on. He talked to the room at large but looked directly at the objects of his speech.

Each time my eyes strayed from direct glance back to the glass of wine, he figured the point of his words was being missed. With this he sidled up closer until his thick eyelashes brushed my face. Among happy, healthy and eagerly com-municating folk everywhere in southern Europe, there is a rule: if the stranger can't understand, try harder; get closer, move right up, look him in the eye and. . .YELL!

Exhausted by so much ardor, flummoxed by Portuguese wine, we bowed to the host, his wife, the woman at the bar, all the friends and cautiously backed out hoping our efforts at polite gestures had come across.

Chaves Campground

Laughing, we drove on to the small but neat campground at Chaves. The Portuguese like camping and spend summer weekends fleeing from factories and offices, shops and mar-kets so as to be near the beach or in the mountains.

An English-speaking manager showed us to a numbered spot. A big crowd of campers strolled, talked and visited, drinking tea or wine with their friends. Soon we were caught up in this neighborliness when a middle-aged man, slim and balding, spoke to us in very formal and correct English in-viting us to join him and his wife. He was a news vendor from the university town of Coimbra and was here to take the waters at Chaves spa. We followed him to his tent, sat, sipped wine and relaxed.

Spreading a map, the friendly man described the best areas of Portugal and its most famous sites. "Now here," he touched the map, "is our city of Coimbra. Please do us the honor of a visit." He sketched a map of the city locating his shop near a plaza. What an introduction! We were in Portugal less than two hours and we were befriended and served wine, twice.

Antiquities In Use

The city of Chaves shines beautiful and dirty, bustling and slow-tempoed, with handsome squares paved in marble. The whole town tilts towards the river where a narrow roadway

111

crosses by way of a bridge—a bridge built by the Romans.

None of the Portuguese are amazed to see a two thousand year old bridge that, aided by the additions of rickety iron railings and a slather of asphalt for road surface, still carries the main central Portugal-Spain traffic. In any other country a steel and concrete structure would have replaced this marble one. The Portuguese regard time as instantaneous. They accept ancient structures right alongside of modern ones and make little fuss over either. They don't try to embellish or hide them in a flurry of pride or shame. Hundreds of years of artifacts are accepted as natural bits of the landscape not worthy of note. "That house (medieval palace) over there is uncle so-and-so's; that (13th century Gothic) church is where I worship," a man mentions as causally as someone else would speak about his ten story modern apartment building.

The Portuguese sense of history is so strong that the antique is accepted as part of "what is" instead of something precious and remote. Here the farmer thinks nothing of building new farmhouses of rough cut granite in slabs big as bathtubs, the same methods their ancestors employed a very long time ago. It's easy to envision a host of unemployed pyramid builders leaving Egypt 3000 years ago to go to Portugal to erect granite houses and beget more stone masons. A close examination of these perfectly maintained houses will not reveal which are five years old and which are 500. Nor do their occupants care.

Portuguese Constabulary

Just as we thought we had a handle on this rural part of Portugal we drove into a small city. Directing traffic was the usual small town cop standing at the center of an intersection waving his arms at cars that passed by unheeding. His grey uniform was freshly washed and ironed but sagged like a tent, and his shirt bulged over his overhanging belly. Nothing surprising about him; he could have stepped right out of any intersection back home.

Down the street we double parked and started to get out. At this moment, a different cop stepped up to ask us to move on. She was far from usual; her uniform was made of grey stuff but her skirt was pleated, the blouse fitted carefully to show off her fantastic figure.

Something New Along the Roads

Along the back roads in this part of Portugal are farms utilizing every inch of precious field, where crops are tended with incredible neatness. At crossroads, springs have been tapped to make a watering place. Behind the water-filled troughs, white and blue glazed tile murals decorate a back wall. Driving along these farm roads becomes a visit to outdoor cathedrals where murals depict saints gazing heavenward supported by cherubim tickling their feet.

Portuguese People

There usually are a flock of children splashing beside these sacred roadside fountains. They have so much of the same look as the cherubim on the tile panels—a kind of angelic-devilish glance—that it's natural to chuckle again. They have skin that the sun brushes gold and hair that forms a curly halo. They wave and cheer. Ask directions and they seldom withdraw shyly. Instead, confident grins spread across their beaming faces that erupt with rapid Portuguese while their hands point in more than one direction. On these roads grown-ups take evening strolls, women and men waving and smiling in friendship. These handsome people recall Norse as well as Roman ancestors. Portuguese remind us more of our polyglot American crowds than any "Latin" types. You see faces with straight noses alongside neighbors with turned-up freckled ones. Goodly amounts of long, straight black Mediterranean hair contrast with curly blond and a sprinkling of redheads. Their flashing eyes are brown, or blue or grey. White skin and heavily muscled features range side by side with brown skin and aquiline features. None of these people stand very tall or spread very wide but all have quick, lithe movements.

Marble Mosaics

Ordinary Portuguese sidewalks are made of marble mosaics: black and white cubes forming patterns of vines, garlands and arabesques. You walk a marble carpet leading from one park to the next; the true Portuguese monuments are these delicately patterned walks. In spite of the few pompous statues, it is the mosaic walks and the manicured gardens that catch the eye. The foliage shades from darkest green to yellow greens to grey greens with plants set in baroque patterns. Bordering these patterned beds are spread solid ranks of flowers: yellow marigolds, red dahlias, varicolored roses. You never see a bruised or wilted blossom nor a perennial with a stray branch or an unclipped leaf. And no wonder—armies of gardeners bend at the task of keeping the troops in perfect order.

New Experiences Everywhere

Whether it was the fantastic menus in marvelous small town restaurants along with their strange and delicious wines, whether it was the sense of encountering a gracious and secure people still living a life measured in a 1930's tempo, Portugal thrust upon us a mint-new experience that demands we go back again and again. We laughed then, and we laugh once more remembering. Who could ask for better travel?

ALONE OR IN COMPANY?

Fellow Travelers

Let's suppose you are tempted by the idea of Gypsying. But. . .what about your spouse? Is he or she ready for the great adventure? How would your partner, your dearest friend, your roommate for so many years react to being uprooted and thrust into unknown adventures? How would you like to go alone? Would you prefer it?

At the exact moment you begin to realize the wonderful potential of Gypsying, you may be stopped in your tracks: would it work for the two of you?

Or, if you have a youngster, how would traveling in a threesome work? How could you provide education, stability and routines during such an uprooted life?

One, two, and three, who will go with me? Every venturing group we've met confirms that the initial idea came from one person who set the whole action going. The magical genie rises as smoke from the guidebook, gestures from a river winding in a far away country and whispers in your dreams. He whispers. . .to your ear alone.

Don't be alarmed if you receive very little encouragement from your spouse or other family members. The startling idea of a new beginning, an entirely new life-style, takes time to absorb.

Single Travelers

Though the prospect can be frightening, you may leave a spouse at home while Gypsying. The parting need not be permanent—just a tour away for awhile. Many couples we know who have been married a long time report that such periods of separation rekindle old fires. The traveler's fresh outlook stimulates new topics of conversation, new views on

116

how their future might proceed and often loosens ossified routines.

In the beginning, fear might enter into this arrangement. We've heard people express it in no uncertain terms: "George couldn't possibly go without me. Who would cook his meals and do his laundry?"

or,

"Mary's a bit timid; I have to handle people and tough situations for her. She'd never make it alone."

When the Georges or the Marys return from wandering alone they're transformed into more independent, interesting people. Once this happens, the stay-at-home realizes the tremendous potential travel offers. The next time, he or she may insist on going.

Tales Of Unlonely Hearts

We met a man from California whose wife was content to stay home while he traveled. He was past sixty and retired. He could now take longer and longer journeys stretching from weeks into months and a whole year. He discovered Florence and the city completely changed his life. Here, he said, the amazing freshness and vitality of Renaissance art smote him. He haunted galleries and museums; he read the lives of artists. He learned the principles of composition and theories of proportion and perspective identified by these Renaissance artists. For him, frescoes and paintings came alive and "spoke" with wisdom, revitalizing his view of life and beauty.

Within the last few years, he has become an amateur art historian and a powerful advocate for learning about the genius and development of Western art. He travels alone, yet he is very active, in touch with professional art historians and known and welcomed by museum directors as a charming informal lecturer on his new found passion. His new studies provide the focus and direction that lead him daily while his notes and a growing collection of prints, slides and books fill up his camper.

Meanwhile, his wife has a full life of her own. When he's home from his travels she enjoys his enthusiasm and takes pride in his new expertise. He, in turn, is delighted by her continued involvement in the cultural life of their hometown.

In Mallorca, we met a single woman who makes a living driving a taxi half of the year in Washington, D.C. Her private, special interest is painting, so she spends as much time as possible in Spain enlarging her scope and finding inspiration in the masters of Spanish art. On her jaunts she enjoys absolute concentration without the distraction of friends or relatives. She is not exactly alone; her faithful old poodle goes along too.

Companions Along The Way

When people travel singly, they might discover others of like mind who want to join up. Many rugged-individualist travelers start out strictly alone but find that travel changes them. A single rolling stone can gather plenty of moss.

Even that most stalwart eccentric single traveler, Lady Alexandra David-Neil, who pushed her way into a closed and forbidden Tibet a half-century ago, gathered an entourage as she traveled. Officials resisted her entry, climate and dangers threatened, illness slowed her progress, yet determination eventually carried her right into Lhasa's monasteries and mysteries.

Though starting out on her journey alone, she soon acquired a guide, then porters and eventually quite a band of fellow travelers. She became a serious student of Buddhism, and a scholar of sacred Tibetan texts. After years of study and practice, she was anointed as a lama and continued her journeys wearing saffron robes and ceremonial hats. Then she adopted a young Tibetan Tulku, one born with bodily signs of a previous incarnation as a holy being, and she reared him to be a lama as well.

She started alone. As she passed beyond barriers of race, religion and status she acquired a deep companionship.

Finding A Companion

Most who venture on this trail alone and single, find companions somewhere along the way. A couple of sailors, a widow and widower, separately decided to go voyaging. The lady, in her fifties, sailed from Germany. The gentleman, just turned sixty, voyaged from England. In a small Spanish port, with boats tied up next to one another, they met. Common interests and mutual attraction led to love, marriage and a boating partnership.

Some newly partnered over-forty couples decide to begin their marriage as travelers instead of householders. One happy Maryland couple we know spend half of each year garnering fresh impressions in the Old World. A Canadian couple who we met in Greece only return home for weddings of their grown children or births of their grandchildren.

Marriage Breaks

Not all temporary travel separations work out smoothly. It may be that the urge to go Gypsying masks the desire to escape a relationship.

One traveler we know had been proper husband, affectionate father, successful businessman and pillar of his community. With the children grown he wanted to start traveling. His wife would have nothing to do with such wild goings-on! Buy a sailboat! Set off across the Atlantic! No thank you! So, she stayed at home.

He sailed to England, with a temporary crew. Alone again, he stayed aboard, and cleaned up after the long voyage. With this time for reflection, he realized the separation in distance

symbolized the reality of a marriage that no longer worked. Their long relationship ended with a shattering break.

Our Twosome

The first few months that Megan and I wandered the world together almost wrecked our marriage. In a strange culture, with no friends to buffer our then rocky relationship, and living on very short finances, we had few emotional or other resources to fall back upon. Much like castaways on a deserted island, however, we finally had to make the best of what we had at hand and turned to one another for support, inspiration and affection.

That period, our first Gypsying, became a trial by fire. We came to understand one another at a deeper level than previously. Taking the difficult step of traveling together pushed our relationship to a new and more profound level of mutual understanding and trust. Then we reached a new plane: we found that being with one another, away from the hassles of everyday drudgery, is the greatest fun. We rediscovered the special qualities in each other that had attracted us to one another years ago. We fell in love anew.

Traveling became our gateway to a complete new lifestyle and a complete new relationship. At the end of our first Gypsy journey, we returned home for a few years to reorganize our lives in ways that enabled us to travel as much as we desired.

Your Twosome

Evaluate your compatibility-quotient. You may seek entirely different activities and have different goals. That doesn't matter. Take off, hit the highroad and work out your differences. We know dozens of people who formerly lived together in a kind of armed truce and yet took the chance on travel. They learned that their supposed differences were engendered by the circumstances they lived in. While wandering, they could create their own scene and choose friends and circumstances to suit them better.

Consider your differences: one likes to hike and explore, the other thrives on boulevard shopping. One demands challenging adventures, the other requires "lazy" quietude. Your likes and dislikes in activities may appear to be divisive opposites, yet such polarity can be an asset. During your travels you can each make discoveries in your special areas of interest and then enrich your mate's life by sharing them. We know an enthusiastic sailor who's thrilled to make dangerous ocean passages with rugged male companions. His wife can't stand the open sea. So, she flies to meet him in Normandy, or the Peloponesus or Norwegian fjords where they enjoy each other on quiet day-voyages.

Traveling With Children

To live successfully with your children you must understand their needs as individuals. And traveling requires this too. Leaving home and forgetting school altogether for a year or two can cause marvelous changes in some children. They can gain greater maturity and discover what challenges the world offers. When these kids return to a more conventional school life, they often skip the missed grades and move right to the top of their classes. This is the case with a dozen children we know.

Travel often ignites a new spark in children who had previously been unhappy or who consistently failed to realize their full potential. The chance to experience life outside a limited environment and the separation from poor influences offers the potential for vastly improved self-confidence. The closer ties with parents that can result from long-term traveling together can also provide them with needed courage and inspiration.

Correspondence Schools

Other youngsters require more structured learning such as that given in correspondence courses. The best correspondence schools offer course outlines, textbooks, review and grading of tests in parent-led education. These are economical programs and overseas mailing costs are small. Home-schooling in an intimate family situation provides parents with perhaps their first opportunity to share in their child's true development. [See Appendix J]

Overseas Schools

Other parents opt for enrolling their kids in a foreign school where things are exciting and new. This can shake sleepy scholars into wide awake students. Your library will have a list of American Schools overseas as well as foreign schools who will enroll your child. Tuition ranges from a fraction of the cost of a private school in the States to very expensive as with the posh schools in France and Switzerland.

England's highly structured public school system is neither appropriate nor open to American children unless they start in the very early grades. They make exceptions in the case of students from certain North American prep schools patterned on the British model.

Wherever English-speaking colonies form, private schools open—for example, near American military bases and consulates with large staffs.

A Personal Experience

Traveling with our children was an experience we will cherish forever. We abandoned our structured home-schooling plans after only two weeks in Greece because we realized the foreign experience had far more to teach than any fixed curriculum. Instead, our boys learned Greek culture firsthand

and became friends with the craftsmen and fishermen whose skill and integrity commanded respect. A local tutor introduced them to the Greek language. The ancient ruins stimulated questions. We spent a short time in Turkey and this stimulated them further. Our sons insisted on acquiring historical and cultural information, and thus we began reading and discussing in a free-floating seminar where all of us became students.

When we returned to travel a few years later, our middle son entered a Welsh University for two years and then transferred to the university of his choice. Our youngest son completed his schooling at an excellent prep school in Barcelona and was accepted by five Ivy League Universities. Our sons strongly believe that their European adventures wrought superior changes in their lives, and they now share this enthusiasm as dedicated school teachers.

Another Reward

Traveling together can become a unique opportunity for a closer encounter with your children. Our sons demanded that we be open and straightforward. They insisted we take youthful risks and join their energetic activities. They earned our highest respect with their resourcefulness and strong character. During this experience, they shifted from offspring to dearest friends.

1, 2, 3. . .

Who will go with me? The answer is simple. Whoever will take a chance on Gypsying goes. Be prepared for the biggest and the best changes in personal relations when you hit the road.

DO ANIMALS GO TOO?

Why Not Take Kitty?

Pets are natural traveling companions, yet people say: "I'd love to travel but I have this old cat (dog, parrot, wombat) I love. I just couldn't leave her." Why shouldn't Kitty go along? She'd love to shed her fur in France and Finland and Phoenicia. Take a tip from the Gypsies, take your pets along. One can't imagine a Gypsy wagon clanging down a country road without at least one happy mongrel trotting alongside.

Taking a pet with you need not make traveling more difficult. Most countries welcome animals as the natural accompaniment of families on the move. You can expect to cross borders or arrive at new ports without much hassle.

Of course you don't want to take along a show dog who requires constant grooming, or any other pet that demands you be on constant guard, always tied to his leash. There may be danger in exhibiting pedigreed animals. Flaunting valuables invites theft, so it is better to take along a mongrel friend.

Boats Are Different

Don't expect mature animals to adjust to life on a boat; chances are they will suffer from cabin fever and motion sickness. On the other hand, pets raised aboard boats take naturally to life on the sea and soon become not only the ship's mascot but part of the crew.

Pet Care

Consult your veterinarian on pet health and maintenance and explain that you may occasionally be out of touch with vets. In Northern Europe, there are plenty of pets and good veterinarians. Not so in Morocco and the Middle East.

All the industrial nations abroad have pet shops, and some have familiar brands of foods. Off in the hinterland, though, you will have to prepare your own pet food. We cook up a large pot of rice, mix in finely diced carrots, parsley and ground meat and keep it in the fridge. Our pets thrive on it.

Pet Visas

In the States, in France and all over Europe, entering with a pet is simple. It is more difficult, however, to enter England with a pet. At British Customs, a long arm shoots out, a uniformed voice reads out the regulations and the animala-nongrata is whisked away to be locked up. A poster on the custom room wall pictures a desperate looking rabid dog, hackles up, mouth slobbering, eyes glazed with madness, ready to attack. To think that your old friend who often sleeps on your bed, begs scraps from your plate and keeps your days cheerful could, underneath, be that vicious monster.

Yet the English, God bless their reasonable souls, have provided a civilized alternative. Before leaving for Europe, contact a British Consulate who will furnish forms so that you're met at the airport or dock by a friendly, even kindly, animal-loving customs agent who will take your pet to a government quarantine kennel and return him when you leave England. For this you will be charged a reasonable fee.

But don't think that the English dislike pets. Statistics (can't do without them) show there are more household pets per family in England than any other place on earth. These pets are probably the best groomed, most loved beasts you'll ever see. The foreign pet quarantine is designed to protect these beloved native pets.

Ruffled Irish Feathers

As friendly as the Irish are, they too can be positively difficult about your pet. In addition to the English type quarantine, all birds must undergo an observation period under the supervision of a vet, prior to entering. Requirements depend on the type of bird you intend to bring. Some friends of ours travel with a parrot and had to wait for weeks in France to get the required certification for their bird.

No Visas Required

If you enter any other European country there will not be a quarantine period. All you need at the port of entry is a veterinarian's health certificate, plus a certificate of vaccination. Before leaving home, write the Consulate to make sure of the forms and regulations. Airlines give details for the appropriate shipping cage (most sell or rent them as well).

Bring Your Own

As we were leaving our rented farm house in southern Morocco, we found a sleeping puppy near our van. We were unable to find anyone in the area to claim her.

In Morocco, there's a single breed: spavined, dirt yellow, sniveling curs, the type of mongrel that barks viciously, snaps at ankles and thrashes about in a frenzy of violence until you bend down and reach for a rock. At this gesture, they wheel in retreat and yelp pathetically as though they were being attacked. Our cuddly fur ball soon grew to type.

We called her "Cabra" after the Spanish hoofed creature associated with the devil. With love, care, and good, nourishing food, Cabra developed a scrawny body, protruding hip bones, narrow and spindly shoulders and a pitifully thin chest.

Despite all attempts to train her, the ex-cuddly Cabra became truculent, moody and liable to outbreaks of violent behavior. She tolerated us, even fawning when it suited her plans, but with strangers she was terrible. Let someone ap-

proach the parked van and she would fly into a rage, leap against the glass, snarl and snap. We seldom received unwonted attention from eager hustlers.

Crossed Borders

Crossing national borders in Europe with a pet is normally no trouble at all. Only rabies and distemper shots are required if anyone even bothers to ask. In spite of her going into one of her rages, we crossed France's border with Cabra, and the grandfatherly official thumbed us through with a nod and a weary smile.

Pet Pleasures

A friend of ours always takes her gentle old blind poodle to Spain. She flies directly from New York to Malaga and has only to produce current inoculation papers at the airport. The U.S. requires the same documents. A short time before returning to the States, she takes her dog to a vet for booster shots and the new certificate.

During the flight, her dog is confined to the baggage compartment of the plane in a box-cage, but he eventually forgives her since he is amply rewarded by the months of roaming by her side in the hills and on the back roads. If he had been left behind, Mopsy might have suffered a broken heart.

In an unfamiliar country, a pet is a very good companion. His trusting looks, scent and conversation may carry you through tough times.

Pet Threats

An American couple took their parrot with them on their camping trips throughout Europe. When they crossed one border, a fracas ensued. "Sir, you present two passports only. Please furnish us the third one. I can distinctly hear a man talking to your wife in your caravan." The official was adamant.

"Oh, that's only Perrico," said George. "He doesn't have papers."

"What's this?" the customs man shouted. "Call Police Security immediately! This man is trying to hide a passenger."

Perrico stuck his brilliant green beaky head out the window and squawked, "F___ off!"

CHOOSE YOUR TRAVELING HOME

You Can Take It With You

Imagine a house that moves, that rolls on wheels or slips through the water. You can take it with you wherever you go. It's time to make that first choice: are you going to travel by camping van? By sail boat? By canal boat? it really doesn't matter which you choose first, you can try them all eventually. You will learn the special freedoms and restrictions of each.

Try A Camping Van

People who travel by van swear theirs is the only worthwhile lifestyle. "Look here," they say, "a van gives you unlimited opportunity. Almost every country in the world is open to you. You don't have to worry about storms or floods as you would in a small boat. You just drive inland to escape tempests or leave for higher ground when spring rains overflow the river banks. And such ease, ahhh."

In a van you can collect neighbors and friends and be as sociable as you want to be. You can move in a cavalcade and make camp together. The vans can outline a square like Conestoga wagons with the center space serving as an outdoor parlor and the campfire a place to gather, talk, eat and sing.

On the other hand, vanning can give you all the privacy you desire. You can travel alone in your van and stop at a cove beside the sea, in a lonely site high in the mountains. Or, you can camp in a remote corner of the desert.

A breakdown need not be a hassle because you can retire into your shell and sort out the problem at leisure. You are not forced to find a hotel or look for supplies. You can take your time and fix the problem when you are fresh.

On the highways there's always a potential for traffic problems. Yet experienced vanners ask: "WHY take the main roads and WHY travel in peak hours?"

Hike the Alps! Live in Florence among Renaissance glories! Explore the interior of Spain! Venture into Morocco and over the vast plains of Turkey! A van will take you wherever your dreams lead.

Try A Sailboat

What's that? You've never sailed before? Don't let a little thing like that stop you. You can learn to sail, learn to navigate, learn to live comfortably at sea. In the process you'll realize you still have a lot of potential for living that hasn't been explored before. Don't worry if you confuse port with starboard or a main sheet with a main halyard; the right information and correct moves will become second nature to you.

To get started find a good teacher, then go gently into that liquid world with its quick tempers. If you cherish the sea you will make longer passages like a lover who lingers with his beloved. A Canadian couple we met limited their sailing to the Mediterranean at first where they gained experience with their sturdy Nicholson 32. Over time they handled her in rough storms and navigated the inland sea without getting hopelessly lost.

After a few sailing seasons they had the confidence and courage to go beyond the confines of the Mediterranean. They sailed to the West Indies, through the Panama Canal and on out to the South Pacific. Their postcards from Auckland, Papago and Tahiti describe the beauty of these places, mention perilous situations but seldom touch on the process of sailing itself. Sailing has become second nature to them as inherent as breathing. Within the space of a few years their lily-white innocence has been weathered to a knowledgeable, salt-encrusted hoariness.

Try Canal Boating

In England, there are narrow canals thrusting in and out of woodlands, gliding across meadows and darting between rows of buildings in remote villages. Along these canals English families cruise, mooring against flower-decked banks or tying up their boats inside towns for shopping or visiting. These boats range from small plastic cruisers to steel "narrow-boats" fitted out as complete homes.

On the Continent there are small and broad canals. Criss-crossing the landscape Europe's great canals are major freight routes for industrial and farm products. These canals also hold many canal boaters who make their permanent home on steel barges. The 150 foot steel barges house whole families who have been living like this for generations. It is striking to watch a barge sail by with its decks full of kids playing, bright colored awnings flapping and potted geraniums blooming.

A canal boat enables you to enjoy the privileges and pleasures of village and town without the fixity of place and outlook. In England, the Low Countries, France and Germany canals can also lead you to landscapes and villages not readily accessible by roads.

Checking By Renting

No matter which you choose—you may love a van and loathe a boat—you can learn a great deal by doing a test run in rented equipment for some time before buying.

You may be prone to seasickness and not know it until you've tossed about on choppy seas in a small boat for a few days. The first day at sea on a trial run may leave you feeling queasy, but the second day when the chop has steepened. . . . You can investigate ways to overcome your tendency or. . . give up the sailing idea entirely. If you had the same experience on a purchased boat, you'd be stuck.

Get Experienced Advice

Whichever moving home you chose, get experienced advice. Unfortunately most van literature is written by commercially sponsored writers who are less than totally disinterested. Talk to people who have a few years of back-country van adventures behind them.

The late Eric Hiscock and his wife lived aboard sailing yachts longer than anybody. The Hiscock books form an almost complete "how-to" compendium taking the novice from selecting a boat to rigging it, outfitting it, learning to sail and cruise. Some examples are now a bit old-fashioned, yet these books remain important to the learner.

Other sailing books including those by Lin and Larry Pardey can bring you up to date. Several good canal books published in England will guide you to the better canals and make suggestions about boats. [See Appendix H]

Recouping By Reselling

Depending on the market and other shifts in economic conditions you may resell the boat or van for a reasonable sum. If you sell at a loss, the loss represents a very cheap way of traveling. It will be cheaper than any combination of public transportation except old third-class Turkish buses. During times of wild inflation you may sell at a profit and count the gain as a good bet well hedged.

Acquiring A Boat

If you decide to get a boat, and you know which kind you want, how do you go about buying it with assurance? There are many suitable and seaworthy boats to choose from. Finding boats for sale in remote harbors, estuaries and yards is an almost impossible task. For this you need to contact a yacht agent or broker and look over his offerings. He will show you his catalogue of photos, and when you spot some you like he will take you to see them.

Many fine brokers have led buyers to their dream boat at dream prices and become life-long friends in the bargain. A Dutch broker we know fights for his clients until he's made a deal they could never have made on their own. There are good brokers in England. We know of a piratical looking gent named Morgan on Ibiza Island whom you can trust to find the right boat at the right price.

You'll also need the services of a qualified surveyor, who will inspect the boat and insist the seller make good any defects before you take possession. You'll be sorry if you don't have this survey before handing over your cash.

Acquiring A Van

Buying a van requires a decision: new or used? New ones come complete with factory guarantees but can be pretty expensive. We bought a used van in superb condition from Australians who were returning home after a year of traveling in Europe. They had kept it in top condition; the required maintenance work was done at factory authorized dealers. With used vehicles, however, you take your chances.

In England newsstands carry two used-vehicle sales magazines that list various types and costs of available vans. In Holland, Germany and France, big city newspapers normally have long want-ad sections on vans.

You can't get parts or proper maintenance on U.S.-built vehicles in Europe or North Africa. But if you have a favorite U.S. model you insist on using, it isn't much trouble to ship one on a freighter or to take one aboard the ferryboat from Montreal on Polish Ocean Lines. Check shipping costs before you decide. No European country we know of challenges the standards of U.S.-built vehicles, so they won't hassle you with government safety and pollution regulations.

Our experience taught us that it's much more satisfactory to buy a European van. In Europe, Ford and General Motors make excellent light trucks equipped with small, four-cylinder diesel engines. Mercedes Benz delivery vans that have been professionally converted make the best camping vans with good accommodations and finishes. They're priced about the same as high-quality van conversions of equal size in the U.S.

There are several custom van converters in England that offer a wide range of models and finishes. Instead of leasing, you can purchase one with a buy-back agreement based on condition and mileage when you turn it in. [See Appendix E]

If you want to buy a van very cheaply and are willing to take money-saving risks, you can shop as young travelers do, outside Australia House in London or near the American Express office. Here vans are hawked like oranges and apples.

Along the street are vans with signs in the windows and sellers inside. Of course most have been owned by energetic younger people who splatter rainbow colors over the bodywork and paint signs as various as: "Mother!" "Bombay Or Bust," "African Safari Freaks," "Love Tour Leader." Some of these colorful units can be bought for just a fraction of what they'd cost anywhere else.

A friend bought one of these with the idea that when it collapsed he could abandon it beside the road. After long and satisfying travels it came to its final halt. He removed his gear, hitched into the nearest town and took the train. He had enjoyed that van for a couple of years; now he is many dollars ahead and ready to buy another.

How Big?

Believing you need separate rooms for living, sleeping and bathing, you may want a very big van. Before you purchase a big van rent one and travel to small and charming villages. The great wide van gets stuck between buildings on narrow streets; the long chassis wedges at tight corners. Check the amount of fuel a van-monster guzzles. High consumption can break a budget. Our rule is: 17 mpg or better. Overseas fuel prices can run twice or three times higher than North America's top cost. Prepare to pay two to four dollars per gallon in Northern European countries.

Not knowing better, we rented a big van in London and traveled up the M1 motorway towards Scotland.Very soon, heavy crosswinds pushed the big vehicle around. Fighting the wheel left me exhausted after only a hundred miles. We got off the main motorway onto secondary roads to see the ruins of Hadrian's wall, the boundary between an England subdued by the Romans and the fierce wild lands held by the free Scots. Our route led to a typical narrow tarmac country road. With the van's width we often had to pull off and stop to let oncoming traffic pass and that was not what we needed.

Farther along, the route turned onto the Roman Way, 1900 years old, rough and made for chariots. At we trundled down this bouncy road the stone fences closed in on us. Finally, the walls crowded right against the ancient paving, leaving a narrow track. We could only move at a crawl, and then a sudden screech of metal against stone announced we were stuck hard.

Praying there was no one watching, I dismantled part of one of the walls to set us free, backed up a half mile, got out and rebuilt the wall and then sat utterly frustrated. Megan cheered me up with a spot of British tea.

We were more than willing to exchange that spacious van for a smaller unit. Next we tried a van conversion of a standard panel truck. Although much smaller inside, it promised us unrestricted travel and we could go down any road and into any village. That was the convenience and pleasure we wanted.

Living Small

Larger rigs mean less traveling. To learn to live in the small spaces of vans and boats we had to adopt more coordinated routines so as not to upset one another's activities. We learned the value of companionable silence. We regained flexibility and discovered that perfectly comfortable shelter, delightful dining and adequate storage could occupy very little space and require very little time for maintenance. We lost indoor spaciousness but gained freedom and the leisure to explore. The smaller quarters forced us to regain sensitivity to each other. Soon we felt like honeymooners.

Check The Layouts

Look for an interior layout that will make living comfortable. That sounds obvious and simple, yet a good layout is hard to find. Most ready-made smaller vans and boats are designed to sleep a maximum number of people for weekend trips. Your priorities are different since your moving house need sleep only two or three. You intend to go a long time and a long way.

The storage and cooking facilities of most commercial units are inadequate; you can prepare only snacks or precooked meals. No thought has been given to lengthy use of the van as a self sufficient home. Where do you store a week's groceries? Where do you shove the dirty laundry? Where do you shelve a hundred paperback books?

A sense of spaciousness is vital. You want to enjoy living, reading and moving about without a restricted feeling. Full standing headroom is a minimum requirement: don't begin this new lifestyle with a permanent crouch. The idea is to loosen up and spread out. Any unit you like should be examined carefully. Spend time in it going through the motions of actually living in it. Pretend to cook a meal. Reach for the utensils and foods. Where do you cut something and on what? Which system of storage and multi-purpose surfaces will take the place of spacious cabinets and work surfaces? In the best galley layouts, efficient movements and convenient storage save steps. Indeed, after using a well-organized but tiny galley, few cooks hanker after a big kitchen. These happy chefs develop techniques to prepare gourmet meals.

The best galley design divides the space so that sink, cooker and work surfaces are on one side and the refrigerator, with its storage or worktop, is on the other. This layout encourages a variety of working positions and movements. If the dining table is placed near the galley it becomes additional work space on which to chop, slice and grate. Avoid a tight corner galley (so many are designed that way) where frustration levels peak.

Look at the clothes closet. A usable closet needn't be large; it's amazing how little space is required for a few dresses, a jacket and slacks. It must be long enough so the clothes will hang without touching the floor. There will be times when you will want to wear something other than jeans and knitted shirts. By forfeiting adequate closet space your dress clothes will look as if they've just come out of the laundry bag.

Sleep In Peace

It is essential for the van or boat to have big, comfortable beds, especially a large double-width one if that is your sleeping habit. When complete rest is assured, life takes on a rosier hue. If the bed folds up into day couches, so much the better. You can snatch after-lunch siestas.

Good Standard Units

Consider how daily, moment-by-moment living is going to be housed, equipped and arranged. You'll soon find what works and what doesn't. Fortunately the market does present a few standard vans and boats with good layouts.

A van with a standard light truck body can be narrower and less conspicuous than a widebodied camper. Get your profile down! Keep it low! After all, you're going to travel and seek acceptance among people already suspicious of strangers. Drive something unremarkable.

Cool It

A refrigerator is so important a whole book could be written about it. The best ones operate on either bottled gas, twelve-volt battery current or the local utility current. It will be tiny compared to your home refrigerator, therefore, its location and interior design should be the best available. The better designs have a door panel with place for full size litre bottles, interior shelves that remove easily, sufficient depth for storage containers. If possible, the refrigerator should be raised up off the floor to make access handier.

Gaz It

Van refrigerators and stoves run on liquid petroleum gas (LPG). In Europe and North Africa a built-in tank under the vehicle is a real bother since there are few places to fill them. European vans are fitted instead with loose steel bottles of gas. "Standard" bottles are standard only within the borders of one country. German LPG bottles can't be filled in France, and French bottles can't be filled in Italy, etc., etc. The only universal bottle is the very expensive "Camping Gaz" which most campgrounds, sports shops and marinas in Europe and Africa carry. You turn in an empty for a full one and hand over many times the normal price for gas.

Without a "standard" for LPG bottles you can get around the hassles with a filler-adapter for the particular gas bottles you own. You guessed it, nobody makes filler-adapters.

We decided to do something about this unstandard standard. It took a mere six hours to find a machine shop to create a gas filler adapter. We had to wait only two days to have it made. We paid an arm and a leg to be able to step up to any old butane pump and get a refill.

With our hotsy-totsy, universal filler aboard we pulled into a "Gaz-auto," a service station equipped to fill up the tank of a butane fueled car. I parked the van off to one side, removed the empty gas bottle and carried it to the pump. The attendant took one look and shouted that it was impossible to fill the bottle.

I flourished the spanking new, universal filler. "Here, I said proudly. This is just what you need."

"No signor. No fill here. It is for autos only." And with finality he turned to a proper customer.

Defeated, depressed, I slumped back grumbling my woes. "That's all right," came Megan's bright voice. "Put the bottle in the van through the back door. Now drive over to the pump." I drove.

"Now get out and open the back door and ask for a LPG fillup."

The attendant filled it up. No problem.

Reliable Diesel Power

Consider a diesel powered engine, a small four or five cylinder type which has been produced for many years so that all the manufacturing and design bugs have been worked out. Those diesels run on and on forever with minimum problems. They start with difficulty on cold mornings, they won't push you very fast and they accelerate like balky mules, yet a trusty diesel won't let you down. Also, diesel fuel is usually cheaper.

With a diesel you'll need to take the standard precautions

of cleaning the fuel filters, topping up the oil, having the injectors cleaned and adjusted periodically. An engineer cautioned us firmly: "Don't let anyone tinker with a diesel until it is obviously in bad trouble. A diesel keeps going just fine until it has to be rebuilt entirely."

Popular Trucks

We rolled into a small roadside village in Tunisia traveling in an old Ford Transit van that looked like one of the standard, bashed-in trucks that can be found whirling up dust all across North Africa. Behind the village, stood a hilltop ksar— a six story granary built of rounded, stone-and-mud rooms. These 400 year old structures are fast disappearing in Tunisia through disuse and erosion. The entrance was barred.

The village houses crowded closely together, their multivaulted roofs looking like a baking pan filled with loaves of whitewashed bread. Young men swarmed out to greet us. The women kept hidden. We made our desire to visit the ksar clear by gesturing, grimacing and mumbling a handful of unconvincing French words.

"Of course, stay here for the night. Where you from? You like Tunisia? Welcome, welcome!" French mixed with flailing arms and a smattering of English helped us understand.

Someone stuck his head inside the van and shouted back to the others. "Look at this! They live inside and... all on wheels. Why, it's just a Ford! Could you believe?"

Before long, I was invited into one of the houses to eat supper. This was the normal male invitation. The lady-of-the-van was expected to remain in her truck.

I got out. That was the signal for the women, young and old, to surge out of their houses and invade the van. In all, over twenty squeezed in to learn about the amazing dwelling of the foreign lady. The clothes closet was examined and cooking pots, plates and cups and even books were fondled. What a lot of useless things these travelers hauled around!

Later, Megan told me the women were polite and giggling, even the oldest crone laughed like a girl. They demanded Megan show them her costume jewelry, and in turn, the Tunisian women twisted around to reflect the light off their beads and earrings.

Comparing notes with people who trundle about in big aluminum boxes we learned their vans were too exotic to enable this kind of mutual curiosity to be satisfied. At that village in Tunisia, ours was just another Ford truck stopping by.

A True Gypsy Wagon

If these choices don't strike your fancy you can literally "hitch your wagon" to a horse-drawn caravan. There are still real gypsy wagons: carved and painted, riding on high wheels pulled by a big dray horse. There are plenty of back roads with little or no motor traffic. You'll feel comfortable and untroubled this way.

We met two young Frenchmen who had rebuilt such a wagon and completed a summer circuit around the Brittany peninsula. In Ireland a well-organized company not only rents Gypsy wagons and horses but also suggests routes and provides maps. [See Appendix E]

A horse-drawn wagon adventure is rough for some people. For heat there is a pot-belly wood stove. For sanitary arrangements bushes have been conveniently placed along the roadsides. You can see a beautiful Gypsy wagon on exhibit at Sandy Balls Campground, Hampshire, England.

Journeying Joys

Well-meaning friends and family often argue against Gypsying. Won't travel be filled with troubles? Won't the worst things happen? Of course troubles happen to us as well, yet there is less temptation to sit and mope. The high road calls, new ventures beckon. The very essence of Gypsying drives us to new action, to meet fresh challenges. With the present so vividly, commandingly in charge, a regretful past and a fear-filled future simply do not intrude. Gypsying makes it possible to live fully in the ever renewing now.

It doesn't matter which traveling home you choose—try them all. The most important decision is to start your adventure and continue it. The right way and the right means will come to you. Better yet, you'll find your inner life changes bit by bit. Troubles will no longer become signals for defeat. They will become signals of opportunity.

THE ROADS, THE RULES, THE CONDITIONS

Do Drive

Driving overseas is easy and fun. Highway conditions in Europe, North Africa and the Middle East are certainly different than at home but not so different that you should be concerned. However, one guide to traveling in Europe recommends: "Leave the driving to them," declaring in the strongest terms that it's best to take public transportation and not a rental car. Such advice is written for the tourist with a couple of frantic weeks on the road, not the After-Forty Gypsy for whom travel is a way of life.

Writers who advise against driving overseas cite the high cost of everything: fuel, tolls, tourist-priced repairs. They worry us with warnings about theft, accidents, strange driving laws and larcenous police, none of which have been a part of our experience. We drive a low-profile van that doesn't look worth stealing and doesn't appear to contain valuables. Free from time schedules, we pick off-peak periods for driving and nearly always hole-up on weekends so we don't compete for the short periods of leisure afforded the local populace.

Good Or Bad Drivers?

England introduces you to the best drivers in the world. Yes, they exhibit crazy antics as they charge furiously down razor-thin single track roads in a mad racing stance with teeth agleam, hair blowing and eyes fevered. Most back roads in England are lined with hedges that close in on both sides of the road, reducing space and vision to a minimum. Despite hazardous conditions and cavalier attitudes English drivers are prepared to brake efficiently and give way to all oncoming traffic by ducking into pull-offs. Old-fashioned courtesy and modern skill show in the way English drivers wait patiently at pedestrian crossings, come to full stops at intersections, obey detailed traffic regulations and maintain the lowest incidence of traffic accidents anywhere in the world.

France glories in its wide, beautiful main super-highways: the Autoroutes. This fantastic freeway system leaps from the Mediterranean to Paris, from the North Sea to Paris, from anywhere at all to. . . Paris. Yet Autoroutes transform the ordinary French urban driver into a racing fiend. Having escaped from the city, he unleashes his frustrations like a kamikaze pilot seeking death-glory. Junctions near Paris are France's major highway problem. At these merges, crushing streams of four lane on-ramp traffic plunge into six lanes of bumper-to-bumper rolling steel bombs. The inning-and-outing, the screeching, the metal scrapings, the bleating horns from left and right gradually set you up as the next victim. Merges display the French driver at his height of creative destruction with pile-ups of at least sixteen autos involved in each accident.

In France, we take the excellent secondary roads and hardly bother with the merges. Many have crossed and recrossed France without mishap by lingering along back lanes with slow speeds, good paving and a manicured landscape neat as a private garden. The small-town French driver is as courteous as his English counterpart. When we use the Autoroute, fifty miles from Paris we turn off and get on the back roads.

European drivers must pass rigorous tests to get their licenses. They are not about to lose them by disobeying laws or by careless driving. The general level of driving competence is high.

Europe's Good Roads

Driving aficionados have yet to find a truly terrible main or secondary road in Europe. After all, the continent has had centuries to upgrade the donkey trails and cow paths, and European farmers insist on good paving to take their produce to market. In Holland the roads are better than excellent. The Dutch have improved upon the finest U.S. standards of design and construction: their highways are works of art. Except for those few mountain roads that are best left to hikers and mountain goats, Spain's roads invite you to tour.

Third-World Roads

Main roads in the Middle East, Turkey and North Africa range from fair to ghastly. Often, daytime driving is halted by a flock of sheep adrift on the paving like snow. For those who foolishly insist on driving at night, be warned of potential disasters. It's normal to encounter wandering cattle, unlighted bicycles and horse-carts—even men asleep in the middle of the road. Sign the pledge to never, never, never drive when daylight begins to fade; do this and many Third World driving worries will evaporate. Add to this no driving during rainy conditions, and you will fully enjoy traveling in these countries. The only hopeless driving situation we know occurs on the main truck route across Turkey to Iran. Bulldozers daily push miles of newly-demolished vehicles off onto the shoulders. Without the daily push, the road would be permanently blocked.

Those Tempting Speedways

Some highways are so good they tempt us to whoosh straight past every important place we should stop to visit. German Autobahns streak a conduit through stretches where the mountains and rivers should make you twist, turn and look around. The only indication you're in Germany is the controlled roar of the outside lane with its grey blur of Mercedes.

Driving Permits

A current driver's license from your home state suffices in

Europe if you drive your own vehicle. Your passport and a green card documenting foreign insurance coverage will be requested at borders. Often in European Community nations, the border guard will only be interested in your gracious smile.

The American Automobile Association issues International Drivers Licenses but these are hardly ever required. We have crossed Morocco, Algeria and Tunisia, driven in Greece, Yugoslavia and into Turkey and have crisscrossed Europe several times without once being asked to show our I.D.L., or any driver's license at all.

The International Driving License is important, however, if your insurance company considers it so. Bring the issue up with them since they won't mention it otherwise. If needed, you must get an I.D.L. before you leave the U.S. They are good for one year. It's possible to request the AAA to mail a renewal upon reapplication. The I.D.L. is also required at rental agencies.

Since most U.S. driver licenses expire after only a few years you may want to apply for a British driving license which is good for twenty years. To do this you will have to take a driving course from a certified English driving instructor.

Even if you've been driving for decades, there's plenty to learn in an English driving school. They teach careful, alert driving techniques including a whole new attitude towards shifting and keeping the car in constant control. Hours of instruction include a complete rethink of too-familiar driving habits and a full introduction to European driving regulations and road sign systems. When you complete the course, driving on the "wrong side" in England will be only a minor peculiarity.

License Plates And Registrations

European license plates have no annual dating, and a nonresident's car is not taxed. You'll see 15 year old English vans cruising the Continent with rusting plates that haven't seen

149

the inside of England in that amount of time. We saw an Ohio plate with no date, no number, nothing except praise for the Buckeye state. No one questions such oddities as it's normal for the original license to travel permanently with the car.

Auto Insurance

Check U.S. insurance companies for auto insurance rates abroad; they are usually two to three times more than British Insurance. For British Insurance you will need a British home address (but not in London where insurance rates are astronomical). Allow six weeks for processing. Your British friends might let you use their address to get excellent rates.

About half the British insurance companies will welcome you. The other half will not even consider your application on any grounds—and with good reason. An agent recounted his company's horror story to us. It has burned deeply into the British insurance consciousness. His company insured an American gentleman who traveled through Europe only to meet with an accident in which his wife was severely shaken. The wife sued the husband and his insurance company for his negligence. She collected, and they remained married and apparently compatible. This sounds pretty ho-hum in our litigation-crazed society, but it raised a scandal, and insurance rates, in Britain.

Legal Papers

Carry all your auto documents with you in case of an accident. Hide the original and flash a good photocopy. If some official falsely accuses you of unspecified and unanswerable crimes (as sometimes happens) and snatches away the papers in an attempt to limit your movements, you can always thrash about, moan, turn away in despair and. . .escape across the border with your original ownership papers in hand.

Repair Tools And Parts

Put together a small kit of break-down tools and spare parts. An alternator, fan belts, spark plugs, fuel injectors and other such common replacement parts can be hard to find in remote villages. It's worth the peace of mind even if you never use them. Include a very easy-to-use lifting jack and a big "X" wrench for changing wheels. Tire repair service is seldom offered near the places where you have a flat.

We have driven over fifty thousand almost trouble-free miles abroad with many delights and adventures. We only replaced an alternator and headlight bulbs and tightened fuel injectors. And, oh yes, we wore out two sets of tires. We anticipate more driving and recommend it to others joyfully.

Boat Papers

The requirements for boat papers vary widely from country to country. Because he doesn't know the legal requirements of your own nation, an individual Port Captain won't demand much identification. As of this writing a foreigner buying a boat in Europe won't register it because he is not a citizen of the country where the transaction occurs. All you need to show ownership is a properly notarized bill of sale on an official-looking form. Be certain it shows your name and a European address, the boat's name and some number that identifies your boat. Officials have blank forms to fill out; give them plenty of information to fill up the blanks and they stay happy.

The owner of a British boat moored alongside ours in a Spanish harbor for a winter lay-over had trouble with the Port Captain. He had no ownership papers to show. Daily, the official came by to demand, "Either deliver proper papers to my office, or leave the port."

We had a book of Her Britannic Majesties Stationary Office blank bill-of-sale forms on board for emergencies. At

Mike's request, we filled out a form for him. Then we sat back to look at our handiwork.

"Something doesn't look right," Mike said. "The form's okay, you've filled in all the blanks, but what about a signature — and this empty circle down here?"

We looked, and sure enough, the big paper didn't appear convincing. I got off the boat, went to town to make a few purchases and returned. Onto the empty circle, I fixed a bright purple dress ribbon with hot sealing wax. With a large British copper penny borrowed from Mike, I impressed the Queen's image into the fresh wax.

As a flourish, I scrawled the most honorable signature I could think of: "George Washington." The Port captain accepted the document with delight and made a photocopy to hang on his wall.

Official Boating Hassles

Since 1979, Spain and France have tried to insist that all foreign yachts stay in expensive marinas. In France they have even tried to impose a special retroactive "tax." Nobody we know has been willing to pay it, especially since the amount can sometimes equal the total value of the boat. Boating friends have found a way to avoid the payment and also stay in such ports at minimum cost. First, they never stay too long at any one place, and they anchor out in a corner of the harbor or tie up alongside fishermen. In so doing, they try to become invisible. And second, they've also discovered a few reasonably priced marinas in need of business; these marinas see to it that the tax man doesn't come around.

The southern canals of France lead inland from the sea to small villages where the villagers are friendly and welcome a boater's trade. Europe's Rhone River is the major waterway for boats into the Mediterranean. At the entrances at Agde and Sete even sailboats can go inland for good distances. We know boaters who have spent months there unmolested.

Safety In Canals

Traveling on canals is by far the simplest mode of transportation in terms of laws, dangers, border crossings and the like. Canal boating is slow and safe from extreme weather and navigational hazards. You can reroute during the annual spring and fall floods when waters seldom remain high for more than three weeks.

When canals have to traverse landscapes with hills, water is trapped in stair-step ponds which have operable gates at each end. The gates and impounded waters are called locks. A boat going uphill enters, the rear gates are closed, water is flooded in to raise the level to the next higher locked pond. The process may have to be repeated in a series to bring the boat either up or down to the desired canal level. While Holland's canal locks only have to raise a boat a few feet from one level to the next, France's hills demand a series of locks that stair-step a great distance.

In France's Canal des Ardennesy we had to work through 27 automatic locks in one day to climb up the several hundred feet to reach the wooded top. After tightening and loosening ropes, tripping the lock mechanisms and trying to beat the timed openings, our muscles were sore for days. Locks are a memorable challenge whether they're the thousand foot long ones on the big commercial canals or the tiny ones leading into canals maintained for pleasure craft. We remember helping French lock keepers hand-crank rusty mechanisms and assisting Dutchmen pole open antique sluice gates. This gave us the chance to meet and work with other boaters and lock keepers. When planning a tour of European canals, get acquainted with the regions you think you may like and the condition of the waterways by reading the literature on specific areas. [See Appendix H] Some older canals have been abandoned; some areas are good in the winter; others are filthy industrial canals that should be avoided. Given the right conditions, canaling provides a chance to explore Europe from an unusual perspective.

Rules Of Canal Boating

You may officially stay in France on a canal boat for six months without concern for taxes; an unoccupied boat may remain for an unlimited time. Some countries have no enforced restrictions. Despite occasional restrictions, many people live aboard permanently. To do so, they keep a quiet and unobtrusive profile and bring welcome business to towns where they tie up. They stay away from their preferred mooring with occasional cruises and preserve the fiction of being out of the country. The most successful boaters avoid envy, project a genuine love for their fellow-man and are welcomed and treated fairly all over Europe.

Turkish Twist

The roads, rules and conditions vary within countries as well as from country to country. Don't judge a country by its cities; explore the countryside before you get discouraged.

We had enjoyed Istanbul's faded elegance and lingered in its huge Oriental bazaar. We'd walked streets lined with crumbling buildings, peered into the old underground vaulted water cistern, visited Topkapi Palace and the Blue Mosque. Yet a week of frequenting tourist sites in a place that once had been the center of a great empire was more than enough big city experience for us. The crowds, the filth, the hustlers finally appalled us. We wanted out fast.

But to our surprise when we began Gypsying in rural Turkey on the enormous Anatolian plain we met small town merchants and visited farm families who were entirely different from the pushy city citizens. We came to more Hellenic temples and ruined cities than we did in Greece. The countryside was populated with gentle people who gave us a more generous welcome than almost any place else we'd been. We tried its few campgrounds and felt content and safe free-camping. Our visit lengthened into weeks.

Roads weren't the greatest, but then we weren't in a hurry. Mechanical problems with the van were repaired quickly and at ridiculously low prices. Highway and village police were courteous and helpful. Diesel fuel was readily available and cheap.

Thinking back, we remembered why we hadn't Gypsied in Turkey before. We'd had a free-floating anxiety about that country compounded of poor and inaccurate news accounts, old Hollywood movies showing Mogul Emperors bashing a-cast-of-thousands, images from who-knows-where of such exotic and unfriendly goings-on that a civilized traveler wouldn't dare venture into such a risky situation. Suppose Ghengis Khan's hordes were to swoop down on our little campsite? Suppose we were whisked off to the deepest bowels of a filthy dungeon for imagined offenses? What about the mysterious Moslems hiding behind veils and wrapped in turbans? What if? What if?

The reality of sunny, bright Turkey with its ease of travel and courteous treatment dashed all our fears and replaced them with warm and friendly expectations.

As with rural Turkey, travel in Europe, Africa and the Middle East is amazingly uncomplicated and pleasurable. Requirements are simple and flexible for the welcome visitor. Don't be put off by unfounded fears and misinformation. Go and learn the happy truth.

CAMPGROUNDS

The Camping Option

When you stay in a city and when you camp in certain countries, expecially Morocco, use campgrounds instead of free-camping. A good rule to follow, whenever you feel the least queasy about spending the night some place, look for a campground instead of an otherwise unprotected spot. And while you're there, catch up on laundry and bathing.

How To Find Them

The tourist bureau at most border posts will furnish you with a campground guide for the whole country, or their central tourism office will mail them to you on request. These campground guides show locations, facilities and prices. In these times, always assume the prices have risen since the printing. You can get guides in England from camping associations, commercial publishers and private touring clubs covering most of Europe and parts of the Middle East. [See Appendix H]

Pay a call to the two automobile association offices in London (The Royal Automobile Club, The Automobile Association) for a total menu of information and road maps. Booklets on the British Isles describing historical, scenic or gastronomic camping tours can be found in London specialty book and map stores. There are books about European campgrounds published here in the States.

For Europe, North Africa and the Middle East, camping trade associations publish lists and more lists of campsites available; yet when driving around, you'll discover, right next to the listed ones, more sites that haven't advertised. Follow the road signs showing a trailer silhouetted against a yellow background or a picture of a tent above an arrow.

The Good, The Bad And The Ugly

Get advance information on campgrounds if possible since they vary so much in facilities, in cleanliness and especially in ambience. Other caravaners are your best source of information. The talk sooner or later gets around to the subject of campgrounds—which ones to avoid and which ones are recommended. It's not often that these tips go wrong; they usually lead to excellent installations you would never otherwise find. The Official Tourist Information Bureau Camping Ground Guides describe amenities but not atmosphere. For Spain, Italy, the Middle East and North Africa, it's absolutely imperative to talk to another on-the-road Gypsy.

In North America there is a huge difference between a scenic campground high in the Rockies run by the Forest Service and an urban resort campsite designed to encourage a long stay. It's a trade-off: in one, the superb forests, the views, the fishing override any other consideration since the amenities may be slim or non-existent; in the city, luxurious facilities may overlook a grim vista.

This is pretty much the same with camping in Europe, North Africa or the Middle East except that even at their luxurious sites there are no utilities available at the individual sites. There may be electric service points dotted around. There are, however, always faucets, and sometimes a central shower/toilet/clothes-washing facility.

Municipal Campgrounds

Municipally owned campgrounds are located in cities with the greatest tourist traffic. Except in Portugal, they are only open during the tourist season. Camping-Michelangelo in Florence, Italy, is a typical public site open from May through

October. You'll also find them dotting France's Brittany Peninsula. Unfortunately, only a few of Spain's cities have them; Cordova is a welcome exception.

A typical municipal campsite is designed on the supposition that most campers will use tents;therefore, they have a service block near the center of action. One end of the block holds a series of dish-washing sinks and sometimes crude kitchens with lots of counter space for setting up portable cooking stoves. The other end of the block is designed for clothes washing (in sinks) with a fenced drying yard beside it. In between, ranks of wash basins, flushes of toilets and sluices of cold showers await the morning rush hour.

Plusher sites supply hot showers provided you get up before dawn to beat the stampeding hordes before they drain the last warmth from the storage tank. At Marrakesh, Morocco, a clever futurist had the foresight to install solar collectors to take advantage of abundant sunshine. Another planted evergreen trees to shade the shower blocks from the fierce rays. Unfortunately, they shade the solar collectors as well.

Sometimes a municipal campsite is set up solely for restricted summer use with a large field mowed to a smooth surface set about with trash cans and water faucets. This is the case in Amsterdam where the stadium grounds makes use of the showers and other plumbing facilities installed for the athletic season. This delightful setting provides space for a thousand campers. Rows of tall trees surround every field and the campground is well served with public transportation.

In the Moslem Holy City of Kairoain, in Tunisia, a small part of the local stadium grounds has been set aside for campers all year long. Finding the plumbing facilities there (in a nearby school building) becomes a strange game of hide and seek for anyone to enjoy. Southern European campgrounds treat electrical power as if it were too precious for actual use. Electricity has come late to these parts and the locals remain in awe of it; not a bad thing considering the utility rates they have to pay. Making an electrical connection in their campgrounds is not easy since each one has unique electrical outlets with a shape, size, number of holes, spacing of holes and so forth not matched elsewhere.

Determined not to be outfoxed, we equipped ourselves with more than fifteen different kinds of plugs and adapters. Nevertheless, at an Italian campground we found an outlet that stumped us. Fortunately the manager came to the rescue. He demonstrated with the aid of a knife that by stripping the connecting plug from the extension cord, inserting bare wires into the live outlets and apparently shutting out thoughts about the lethal 220 volts, a connection could be made. Oh, and we were to secure the loose wires with match-sticks. When it came time to unhook we were treated to a sonic boom and brilliant fire-works.

Portugese Municipal Campsites

Because Portugese municipal campgrounds are close to population centers, have cheap rates and no time limits, Portugese families often haul in trailers and install them with extension awnings, fences and even attached greenhouses. Weekends, Portugese migrate from their crowded apartments to the lush parkland. Some come "home" to the campground every night. Several sites were planted with extra shrubs, strung with lights and arranged with garden furniture. Despite the heavy use, there are always a few spots left for us Gypsies. Besides, the Portuguese are such warm, friendly people that camping in this crowd is a pleasure and a chance to get to know them.

Seasonal Campgrounds

Like most businesses, privately financed campgrounds

range from stark simplicity to luxurious elegance. During the summer months, entrepreneurs set up camping sites along ocean, sea, lake, and river shores. Anywhere that water tempts people out of clothing into near nude-freedom, camp-grounds abound. So you can be sure you'll discover plenty of sites on the coasts of the Atlantic and Mediterranean.

Come the first of July, beaches sprout fenced enclosures to block strong breezes and the sun. People, their gear, tents, trailers, and vans run wall-to-wall.

In one such camp on the Costa Brava of Spain (only a mighty brave idiot would plunge into that icy water in early summer) tents sit so close to one another they actually touch. Campers return here every year, camping cheek-by-jowl with last year's neighbors to re-establish their summer communities.

Here there are also permanent setups, and the facilities and landscaping rival elegant estates and invite long stays. They too become perennial vacation places, but also welcome Gypsy travelers. Along the Mediterranean coast of Spain from Almeria to Gibraltar, high mountains reaching almost to the sea block winter winds and create pockets of warmth on the shore. All along here campgrounds operate year-round and some boast banana trees and other tropical flora. From here you can drive inland gaining altitude quickly so that within a couple of hours you reach snowline. Of course during the winter no matter how warm the sunny camp is the sea runs cold. Despite this, Germans and Scandinavians flock here during Christmas holidays to gleefully plunge in. We get goose-bumps just watching. A few camps insure you get all the sunshine you can soak up, but they insist you camp com-pletely nude.

European Vacation Periods

For an entire month, first Germany then France closes down—whole industries shut tight—while everyone takes a vacation. The campground proprietors stock foreign food specialties such as German sausages and French cheeses. We stayed the night at a French campsite and were delighted to see a bakery truck unload fresh hot croissants and brioche in the morning. To avoid "German Month" and "French Month," don't go to tourist sites.

Private—Not For Visitors

The only way to know if a campground is private is by asking. They set up their own rules and sometimes are the location of a second home: tents and trailers move onto the sites to remain there permanently. Quite a few have no room at all for transients. The ones that do, in off season, make gloomy ghost towns with trailers shrouded in protective plastic covers. All the lustre of good maintenance, summer foliage and frolicking children is gone. Only the thin, lonely cats, scavenging for scraps, remind you of the bustling crowds now absent.

The Very Best

Occasionally individual campgrounds are located in ideal settings, contain near-perfect individual sites and have been maintained in shiny-new condition. Such places entice the most discriminating traveler to linger and luxuriate. One of the best is Las Palmeras in the Moorish city of Elche, near Alicante, Spain. A thousand years ago, the Moorish invaders discovered this region had the perfect soil and climate for growing dates. Las Palmeras Campground sits in the midst of an extant date plantation, a strange and silent place where ringed trunks rise majestically out of white sandy soil. Here neat driveways lead to sites under the slashed shadows of date fronds rustling high overhead. Las Palmeras boasts a camp store, disco, formal restaurant, flowering shrubs, large sunning terrace and a sparkling clean swimming pool. And a shower block flaunts blue and orange tiles, and gushes hot water in shower stalls big enough for two. At least half the campers spend winters here and make day trips to Moorish palaces, Medieval castles and troglodyte villages which are all within a hundred miles.

Permanent Motorhome Sites

On the Cote d' Azur of Southern France there are campgrounds selling permanent lots. Here you'll find large motorhomes or trailers parked on shelves cut out of the mountainside amidst lavish landscapes with paved terraces. Far below the mountain lie numerous old villages and the Mediterranean sparkles in the distance. Some travelers found the place too tempting, bought a site and gave up traveling for good.

Camping British Style

Each country has a slightly different campground style. The Caravan Club founded seventy five years ago was the first English campground organization. It set out to establish plain, neatly maintained fields in rural areas so that its members were assured of a stopover while traveling in England. They have kept to the original tradition: simple, almost undeveloped turfed sites, many adjacent to streams. Each has trash facilities, one or two water points and a fenced waste dumping point.

Caravan Club members have no heart for such frivolities as plumbing and electricity. At CC sites we feel like pioneers who are not about to trifle with flapdoodle modernity—well-bred and neatly-trimmed, but pioneers nonetheless. When you arrive, you notice other campers keeping a distance (minimum spacing rules ensure this) and a discreet quiet. It's as if Lord Whosis had been so kind as to allot a piece of his estate for a bit of jolly old camping. And you're expected to reply to his courtesy with an equal amount of decorum. In fact Lord Whosis and other owners of stately homes do lend sections of their land to the Caravan Club from time to time.

In England some of the bigger, private campgrounds remain open all year and advertise holiday places, meaning there is more to do than sit out of the rain in your camper and drink tea. There might, for example, be pony or horseback riding or archery.

Camping In Greece

On those islands with drive·on ferry boat service there are campgrounds to suit a variety of tastes. The fanciest ones are run by the Greek National Tourist Organization with sites in Macedonia and the Peloponnese. Yet we like best the privately run camps on Crete where historical and archeological sites lie right next door. There are good campgrounds all over the island but it's always a good idea to walk in first and inspect them before you commit. At Kinikadasos on the eastern edge of the island about 70 miles from Agios Nikolaos, an unexpected grove of date palms shades one of the finest sites and a sandy beach.

Turkish Delight

Farther East, Turkish entrepreneurs have begun to set up campsites near all the important archeological areas. Especially good are those near Goreme in Cappadocia, where fruit orchards have been transformed into beautiful sites. Since this is a new area for campers there are usually plenty of spaces available. Above the fantastic landscape of Pamukkale, where a city of stone tombs broods next to a hot mineral waterfall, a motel has provided grassed parking spaces for vans. Their hot mineral baths, despite their rusty appearance, soothe a driver's ache into forgetfulness.

Moroccan Adventure

When the cold clamps down on Europe, many think Morocco the best Gypsy place—inexpensive, colorful and mysterious. Their city campgrounds have the amenities which make a long stay comfortable. On approaching these campgrounds the government's priorities become apparent: first a guardhouse and then a platoon of soldiers and then a handful of policemen with weapons at the ready. You pass through this army to get to the reception office. Inside the camp itself, high walls and barbed wire fences close it off from its surroundings. Despite this touch of grimness, the sites are large, shaded and reasonably well cared for. Since no native Moroccan is allowed inside a camp you won't be bothered with the usual vendors and hustlers looking to conclude a shady deal.

"Character" Campgrounds

Every campground has its reputation for the kind of people it attracts. Amsterdam-Olympic and Florence-Michelangelo campgrounds shout "youth" even though they also have older campers. We always learn something from these bright, busy students who are making contact with others from every corner of the globe. In Florence's campground parking plazas sits every sort of odd vehicle. Refurbished London double-decker buses and old German army troop trucks disgorge laughing, jostling youth arriving anywhere from Australia to Zulu-land. They fling down gear and erect clusters of tents, unfurl national flags and string up long lines of washing. Pretty soon they gather at the terrace cafe to eat, guzzle wine, sing and begin orgies of letter writing. "Dear Mom, we're going to visit the Duomo tomorrow" (if she wakes up before noon); ". . . a pretty quiet trip" (the noise level has hit 100 decibels with juke box, laughter, screams, guitar-whanging). "Will write more later. Oh, guess what, I just met this nice guy. . . ." It's good entertainment and even inspiration for us, though we do park our van in a far-off, quiet corner.

Florentine Opera

The people scene is occasionally highlighted by something special: into the space next to us in Florence glided an ancient, polished vehicle towing an equally ancient and elegant trailer. Slowly and grandly this venerable rig came to a halt with every bit of paint and chrome gleaming as if fresh from the showroom. Out stepped an elderly Italian gentleman, cream colored summer suit freshly pressed, long dignified white hair brushed back, great hooked nose preceding him.

Majestically he bowed, asked did we speak Italian? French? Austrian? Receiving all negations he smiled the smile of infinite charm that can only arise from a soul deeply at peace, shrugged mightily and proceeded to make himself understood in an international patois that rang clear as a bell.

"You are staying long? Leaving tomorrow perhaps? Ahhhh. . ." he said, "I occupy this same spot every year," indicating time reaching back into infinity.

His charm made me feel like a terrible interloper, a thief of favorite spots even though this was our fifth stay over the years. Just as we bestirred ourselves with some embarrassment, he made a gesture perfect for a major performance at La Scala and dismissed the idea. "Never mind, the spot just beside you will do very well. Just a little leveling." This last he indicated should take no greater engineering than entrenching the Suez Canal. More smiles, a restarting of the grand conveyance, and gradual backings and fillings followed.

His charm would have made anyone eager to be of service. With gestures, we indicated a willingness to help push and pull the now unhitched trailer to its desired and exactly calculated spot. He acknowledged our sincere offer to help as true friendship, but he let it be known that he, working alone,

could accomplish all the wonders needed. We retreated to watch.

He pulled out jacks, levelled his trailer to a superb exactness. Next, he snapped open a folding bicycle, brought out a dining table and a padded chaise. All this he shaded with a bright yellow umbrella supported by an ornamental metal stand and enclosed this sitting area with grass mats hung from lines between nearby trees. The whole site was covered in silvery olive trees yet this gentleman required more landscape color, so once again he plunged into his trailer extracting bright pots of geraniums and nasturtiums which he set on his little stage.

The dramatization was awesome especially as he accompanied every movement with little snatches of Italian opera or bits of private monologue and jokes. Then he caught himself, turned to his silent audience and emitted a self-deprecating laugh.

The action kept up this pace for two hours and made us forget a movie we had planned to see. Who would have wasted time in a movie anyway, with this live scenario available?

He completed these preliminaries by raking his new front piazza and sprinkling it with cooling water. He tossed a neatly encased roll of TP into the bicycle basket, sat astride the machine and pedalled off to the WC. End Act I, Scene 1.

Scene 2 opened at the dining table where our hero busied himself arranging things—gleaming china, candles in bronze candelabra, polished silver—all the while humming Verdi like a happy waiter. Satisfied, he slung a broad linen napkin under his chin, tucked it into his shirt and enthroned himself to consume a sumptuous meal with appropriate gusto. We looked on with envy, picking at our simple fare next door in the shadows. The scene continued as he paced, smoked a fat cheroot and let the ash form a long, unbroken tail. That done, he turned off the lights, shut the door, and did he or didn't he favor us with a bow before retiring? We sat up debating this as well as asking: Did his bed have silk sheets? An embroidered spread?

Late the next afternoon, the performance opened on Act II. The heroine appeared, center stage, having made her entry from who knew where. An attractive woman maybe ten, fifteen years younger than our hero, was she wife-come-down-on-the-train unable to appear in Act I? Or was she lady-friend-waiting-in-the-wings for the annual assignation? She too turned to the audience (such confidence!), gave a diva smile, a good evening and sank down on a chaise just as grand and soft as his. Where did the props come from? Who wrote the lines? The plot?

All I can say is: "grazie, signor and signora. Dearest thanks for a fantastic performance. Such expert acting! Such elegance! What meaningful gestures!" It has kept us wondering: what if she were really. . .? What do you think he answered. . .? And to think we saw it all at. . . the Michelangelo campground.

BUSTING LANGUAGE BARRIERS

Can I Talk?

Some people say they don't travel and camp in foreign places among unsophisticated people because they can't learn a foreign language. They feel they won't be able to manage even the simpler encounters of buying food or fuel and getting directions.

Even though we both had a block against learning languages, we went to Greece where even the alphabet is different from ours. We couldn't so much as say "hello." Soon we met Greeks who spoke a little English and others who had lived in English-speaking countries long enough to become fluent. It was enough to make us ashamed until we ran into a young Greek man home on vacation from Sidney, Australia.

"Look here mates, don't trouble yourselves over it," he advised in broad accents of "Strine". "I'm no bloody student either; couldn't bother to grind me head that hard. When you gotta eat you soon get the words. It'll come easy. You'll see."

Encounters Teach Languages

To a wise wanderer, every encounter is an opportunity to pick up foreign words. Megan remembers going into her first Spanish food market and pointing at some tomatoes.

"Ah senora, tomates," said the gentle old vegetable vendor. And then countered with "Quanto?" It was obvious from her questioning look she wanted to know how many were needed. "Quiere algo mas?" was asked when she handed over a kilo of the red fruit.

Of course Megan wanted some other vegetables and pointed at them. As each kind was collected and weighed, the name for it was handed over as well. Within a short time, Megan had collected a basketful of words, phrases and a growing confidence with the language. It wasn't long before she greeted the shopkeepers with polite salutations, conversed about grandchildren and other important topics.

Learning became a child's game as she was encouraged, cajoled and applauded. That made it easy as well as difficult. Easy because new words were reinforced with actual demonstrations; difficult since she was being treated like a child. However, she was soon speaking Spanish.

Her eagerness to travel to other countries increased once she'd "grown an ear" trained to pick up and record helpful words.

She took her food buying encounter to France and again began with one vegetable and expanded into French conversation. Italian and Greek proved as amenable to her tongue as their foods.

Anyone can acquire a rudimentary grasp of languages if she or he is willing to appear stupid. Forget your ego. Concentrate on listening, and laugh along with everyone else when you can't make yourself understood. The Gypsy may act the child, cajole and wheedle to get what's needed without losing essential dignity. You can too. Language encounters can be very threatening while at the same time providing unrivaled opportunities. Seize them and it won't be long before you say in amazement: "Not only can I learn languages, I'm becoming a much more emotionally secure individual in the process!"

More Language Opportunities

To develop your ease with a language, seek out a native who is eager to converse. You'll find plenty of blushing young people who yearn to "spit Eeengleesh." They want to practice on you. Turn the tables, make them your teachers.

Of course there is the tried and true fast-track: take a foreign lover. There are, however, certain difficulties with this.

171

Your spouse might, ah...object. And, the vocabulary you learn may not be useful in more formal, polite society. Be sure you are prepared to accept what comes with a language teacher/lover. We met an American lady who was living with a young Spaniard in order to learn the language. She was flattered by his attentions, but one day she was ready to move on. He threw himself into a temper tantrum alternating between black scowls, heel stampings, ominous silences and worse, he promised suicide and threatened murder. Then he softened and told her the bleakest prospect of all: what life would be like...without him. She stayed. And learned Spanish perfectly.

Language Situations

A true Gypsy travels and communicates without trouble in most countries since he grows up having to learn a variety of languages. You, however, may start out not knowing any foreign tongues, but when you spend time in a country, necessity makes a good teacher. Watching and comparing words to facial expressions and body language gives you clues about what's being said. Sellers need to make it easy for you to understand and will get across essential words. When your smile signals your willingness, it's amazing how patient and helpful people can become.

When you become familiar with a language, you also become familiar with its culture. For instance, as you learn Spanish, you learn that a Spaniard invites God into every sentence. Thus you're exposed to his culture and history: "Vaya con Dios," "Adios," "Dios mio!" tell you a Spaniard knows another One is listening to every conversation.

Even after you have achieved some fluency in a language you can be easily confused when you encounter a new dialect. On our first visit to Alicante, Spain, I went out of the airport lobby to find a taxi. After my third unsuccessful attempt, I returned to Megan, my face flushed with utter frustration.

"What's wrong?" she asked.

"Either we've landed in the middle of a plague or they're all handicapped."

"What on earth are you talking about? These people look perfectly healthy to me."

"But did you talk to anybody?"

"No."

"You won't believe this," I said, "but it's impossible to understand a word they say. That taxi driver said something that sounded like: 'Thee thenore, aaiy moochaths oteleths en la theeudadth.'"

She laughed. "You should have read your guidebook. They speak the most highly acclaimed of all Spanish accents here. That is pure Castilian."

Fearful Flirtations With Languages

Even though it's scary to try to communicate in a foreign tongue don't forget you have years of well developed communication skills to draw on. And, usually you'll find that the man in the street is more than willing to recognize your three-word vocabulary as a noble effort. He will smile, gently correct your pronunciation and urge another word from you. Meanwhile, he will greet each new success with joy. The softness of the exchange, the kindness of the encouragement, will enlarge your vocabulary almost painlessly.

DRINKING PLACES

The Social Scene

Drinking places lie at the center of male social activity in England, Europe, the Middle East and Africa. I go to pubs, tavernas, kafeneons and tea houses to meet the men of a community. And in summer when drinks are served outdoors, women are welcome. Of course English pubs serve ladies year-round. I sit, order a soda and nurse it for a couple of hours while I listen to tall tales, declarations by community leaders, furious political discussions, dickering over marriage arrangements, local farming lore and plain chatter. Men go there for companionship. Their alcoholic consumption is either low or non-existent.

Such drinking places have no counterpart at home. The North American bar hurries its customers to reorder or leave so as to make space for yet more consumers. High overhead demands a big cash flow. Overseas you're urged to linger and make the place a second home. Overhead is kept very low and the owner encourages steady customers. In the best ones, the proprietor is a family man who lives in the neighborhood. He's also a father-figure for the kids who play in the streets outside his tavern.

Pubs

Go and find a British country pub that is owned by a proprietor instead of a brewery chain. With the Publican in charge there's opportunity to experience an English atmosphere unchanged in three hundred years. Typical pubs have a parlor or "snug" set aside for couples, the "bar" where you go for a quick boozeup and the back room "smoke" with its dart board —a space hardly ever invaded by women.

A workman's path home leads through the pub. In cities

lunch-in-a-pub is routine for young executives. Just as tea is the standard British antidote for any crisis, a pint at the pub is standard celebration for any piece of good news. The old pubs are famous for their centuries-old buildings and are sought out for their atmosphere. Blackened oak beams loom overhead, worn stone flagging floors attest to generations of use, wooden settles frame huge fireplaces, old-fashioned beer pulls dispense from kegs, fresh cider and golden mead flow to the sound of singing.

Chai Khanas

North African and Mideast chai houses look and feel completely different from Mediterranean and European drinking places: there is no alcohol and a hush pervades the hallowed atmosphere. Strictly male-oriented, they tend to be drowsy with languid service to match. In Turkish tea houses especially, prepare to wait, and be certain, meantime, to answer the waiter when he asks: "Do you think the weather will remain calm? Has your journey been safe?" Your smiling pleasantries are passwords to his test and eventually (everything in a Turkish chai house happens in a kind of "eventual" stupor) the chat will come around to tea. The waiter's question, "Would you like some?" comes as conspiratorial whisper. You can also order a dollop of hashish to top the tobacco in a hookah pipe.

Ruins of 13th century chai houses dot the Turkish Anatolian plain. Huge stone caravansaries functioned as grand tea houses as well as hostels for caravans. We visit these elaborately carved Cathedral-like fortresses and imagine what the ultimate drinking place was like.

Our favorite Turkish chai khanas are lightly-framed pavilions with porches and glass doors, latticed alcoves and balconies set in a corner of lush green parks.

175

Kafeneons

Greek kafeneons are cozy in winter with a fireplace where charcoal glows and shishkebab sizzle. When spring blows in, large French doors open, tables sit outside on leaf-shaded terraces and the place takes on an entirely different aspect— more a bower than a bar.

Boys from four years old on up come drifting in to stand beside their fathers and grandfathers, to steal a sip of coffee while silently watching the interminable backgammon games. A timid, silent child enters; he's been sent for a pack of cigarettes or bottle of wine. The proprietor hands over the purchase and carefully picks out the right amount of money from the grubby fist. At times a soccer match blares on the tube and the town's entire male population crowds in to watch.

On remote Greek islands, anti-government dissent enlivens the kafeneon discussions. It's the major indoor sport. "Athens!" I've overheard customers shout. "Same pack of rascals for 3000 years! Trust our islanders. We're the only true Greeks!"

In kafeneons life is timed by sips of coffee, metered by desultory talk, paced by philosophical rhetoric. Like other drinking places they function as parlor, asylum and news source. On the terrace there's a parade: wayfarers alight, campers stop for a hot drink, lonely tourists enter seeking companionship and conversation.

Ancient Greeks

Kafeneons appear in twos. In one, the young men gather. Across the street another holds wizened oldsters with their white heads nodding in deliberations. They gather shortly after breakfast and defend their male fortress until way after dark. When you want opinions, advice, information on anything, wisdom on any subject, check into the old man's kafeneon. Go to listen and inquire of Homer, Socrates and Plato.

Italian Tavernas

Italy's tavernas serve mountains of food accompanied by delicious but inexpensive local wine. No matter how slummy the city neighborhood, how scabrous the building, there is the rustic ambience of a country inn: rough-hewn beams, trellises of artificial grapes, festoons of smoked hams. Red checkered table cloths and the Italian beauty behind the serving counter exude rural charm. Mamma Mia comes out of the kitchen to add her greeting and you know you've returned to the family farm, home again.

At the end of a long, heartwarming evening, a bevy of beautiful women come forward from the kitchen to press your hands and insist you return again. It's impossible to hold back tears.

We've visited the real rural thing, a locanda, where we sat in a garden under an arbor with clusters of luscious grapes dangling in our eyes. Our table overlooked a mossy grotto furnished with stone Madonna and nearby a donkey in a pen, a clutter of pheasants, a trio of milk goats chewing patiently and flashy peacocks strutting as lords of the realm. The vino was fermented right on the premises.

Spanish Bodegas

Spanish bodegas are welcoming, open and brightly lit. They're like warehouses with huge oaken casks lining the walls. From a wooden tap the bodegero may pour a glass for you to drink on the premises or fill a bottle for you to take out. Sawdust covers the floor and informality rules the action. With each glass of wine or beer we're served tapas which may be as simple as a few olives or as complicated as stuffed smoked fish. In University towns such as Malaga and Barcelona certain bodegas cater to students and group singing rings good and loud.

Glorious Tapas

In sophisticated Barcelona, the evening ritual at bodegas is more sedate. Here stylishly dressed women accompany their formally-attired menfolk and move from bar to bar, sampling the tapas of tiny shrimps, curled carrots and spicy potato salad. The air sparkles with bright conversation. How these people eat and drink like this for hours and then have an eight course dinner but nonetheless stay slim and sleek remains the "Spanish mystery."

The Cup, The Glass

You could go to drinking places to. . .drink; there is certainly a variety of offerings. Good pubs tap barrels of dark ale that's at its best in Scotland. Our sons once insisted we try three Northwest Scots pubs one night to sample and compare the individual pubs' rich flavors. Fortunately, closing time called a halt to this enterprise before we finished our research.

Chai, as it's brewed in North Africa, curdles the stomach and the imagination. The cook hacks a hunk from a solid tea brick, throws it into boiling water, pours this thick slurry over fist-sized sugar lumps, thrusts in a handful of fresh mint and serves the cloying syrup in tall, delicate glasses. Be warned of the sizzling heat and the threat of a sugar-high.

The Greek kafeneon serves Turkish coffee but won't name it correctly. Face-powder grind, sugar and water is heaped into tiny brass pots and twice brought to a careful boil. The silty brew is served in tiny cups, and while you wait for the mud to settle and the liquid to cool, you and your companions spin yarns.

The Italian taverna wine is cooled in barrels in stone cellar and brought fresh to the table in two-quart bottles. With ample supplies and little concern for prideful vintage, vino is

treated like drinking water, and yet drunkenness is rare.

The variety of wines served in a bodega spans the Spanish peninsula. Sour red wines from the central hills, thick sweet dessert wines from Malaga, the famous sherries from the Atlantic Frontera region lie in barrels waiting your order.

Drinking Diary

With a mildly-Victorian background and attitude, Megan and I hardly ever enter a North American bar or tavern. Yet we eagerly seek out overseas drinking places. They provide us a close-up look at people and customs. Take that afternoon on the terrace of a Greek kafeneon when three teenage girls arrived with a large cake. Solemnly they passed from table to table serving slices to the men who said something quietly to the girls, accepted the cake and left some money on the cake tray. These were orphaned daughters enacting a ceremonial remembrance for their father who used to frequent the place. This was a way for the old cronies to help support their departed friend's children and share memories of him in the midst of his former drinking place.

In the sunshine outside a Spanish bodega we met our first good English friends. Since then we've shared many a worry and abundant laughs on one another's boats and while camping together.

If you do business in a Turkish market, say, dicker over carpets with a rug merchant, you will find yourself seated comfortably on cushions while you are asked the archaic, traditional questions and you will be offered numerous glasses of tea. And as your discussion about price and quality progresses, glasses of tea appear for you miraculously. You arrived as an aggressive customer, but after several glasses of tea, your intention fades into vague emotion. Money? Price for the rugs? None of these mundane matters intrude on this love-feast. You share in the soul of the Mideast. No wonder the

Koran forbids drinking alcohol, it would dull the mystical insight of tea.

Andalucia Magnifico

Andalucia is Spain's old-South, a region that still remembers its difficult victory 500 years ago, when the hated Moor was driven out. That remembrance lies heavy on the Andaloo, yet he can arouse himself and rise to heroics once more at the local bodega.

At dawn an Andalucian Spanish worker lumbers moleishly towards his bar. While the family slept, he timidly dressed, greased his hair, softly donned his beret and fearfully shuffled along to the bodega. Eyes sleepy and cautious, he pushes up to the counter exchanging nary a word with neighbor nor barkeep. In front of him is set a steaming cup of espresso and beside this a full tumbler of brandy. The mole blinks once, picks up the glass and throwing back his head, pours it down in one go. Without a flicker he chases this raw stuff with scalding brew.

Basta! Squinting towards the early morning light, he barks a greeting to his friends, snaps coins on the counter, and steps briskly through the door: Where a mole crept in, a warrior thrusts through the exit, head up, shoulders braced, foot forward in a strut.

Towards the end of day, this tired worker trudges home. He makes a detour through the bodega and there slakes his thirst on one glass of wine after another. He begins to glow, to sing, to stamp his foot and dance. He bumps the counter with his fist, snaps his fingers, clicks his heels and the stage is once more lively with the warrior at play. Yet this comes to an end and next day, at grey dawn, the mole lumbers softly in again.

FEARS, TERRORISM AND NAIVETE

Dealing With Problems

Travel leads you into queer situations that range from life-threatening to hilarious. Strange customs, an offensive immorality, unfamiliar violence of weather or people, threats of rocks and shoals, ignorance, awkward social predicaments, thieves and terrorists—any one of them could stop you in your tracks. Travel involves a lot of wondering about what you should and should not do, what risks to take, how to get out of the fixes that you fall into.

How you handle these problems, how you react, makes all the difference. Knowing a little of what to expect helps. Learning from the mistakes of others (as well as your own) makes life easier. Looking a ghastly or curious situation right in the eye takes out half the sting. Knowing how to affect your own luck removes the rest.

Successful travelers learn to shake off fear and embarrassment and pick themselves up to start over again. Learn to have faith in your own judgement and to accept "impossible" solutions as normal, and miracles as simple reality. Our hard-won motto is: "Laugh and keep on Gypsying."

The Calais Bar

I occasionally am a victim of my own poor judgement and pugnacity. At times, I seem to invite every stupid trap invented and, finding myself stuck, try to brazen it out. Thus I turn a silly situation into something worse. For example, we had arrived at the port city of Calais on a ferry boat one hot summer evening, and ahead of us stretched an endless line of cars inching their way, bumper to bumper, toward the highway.

"Let's get a cold beer," I suggested. From my merchant-seaman days I knew where to find a bar in any port.

Confidently I drove down dingy streets, always turning back towards the harbor. And there, sure enough, a store-front bar blinked with red and green lights. The neighborhood looked a bit rough, but I insisted it was the right kind of place for us.

"Are you sure this is OK?" Megan asked. "It doesn't seem OK to me." She stood frowning at the waterfront dive.

"Oh, come on," I cheered. "Sailors don't care about appearances. They look for really cold beer and a good crowd."

With that bravado, I pushed the door open and we stepped inside. The furnishings did seem a bit odd. There was only one table, and several plush sofas upholstered in gaudy red were arranged around the room. It looked less like a drinking place and more like a Victorian, er. . . house.

We sat and looked around.

With no one to take our order, I strolled over to one of the girls to ask for two beers in my fractured French. When she stood up, her skirt pulled at the seams and stretched over her swelling hips. Her blouse, thin as a negligee, opened all the way down her chest. I croaked my order for two beers and blushed as I went back to Megan. The room's blinking, colored lights cast eerie shadows on the arrival of six dapper gentlemen. "You see," I pointed out, "it's a kind of family place. The way the girls give them such a big kiss. They must be uncles. . ." Megan glared in reply.

Our tepid beer arrived with a bill that was so high that it chilled us.

Paying and heading out as fast as possible, I was confronted with yet another threat. "So you know all about such places, huh? Your merchant navy days, huh?" About an hour down the road her frown changed to a grin and she started giggling.

The Pause That Reverses

During a stroll in the lonely part of a Turkish city a cluster

183

of ruffians suddenly surrounded us. They were tough looking kids without a smile. What could we do? Call for help
where there wasn't an adult in sight? Shout for non-existent
policemen? The number of followers increased and grew into a gang. It looked as if they were ready to. . .! At this moment we remembered to stop and simply grow very still.

Seeing we weren't moving and apparently absorbed in
reading a guide book, they grew bored and dispersed.

When a potential victim stops looking agitated he ceases
to provide amusement; at this point most young toughs move
on. If you can recall your own long-lost youthful attitudes
without flinching, it's possible to summon up a sense of fun,
evoke a laugh and break up the gang-frenzy. But that isn't
always possible.

The Algerian Repulse

We crossed unfriendly Algeria on our way to Tunisia. Night
caught us before we found a suitable camping spot. For safety
we turned onto a dirt road until we reached a cluster of school
buildings in a farming area. We could see oil lamps shining
through windows in the surrounding houses but not a soul
was visible. We parked in a corner of the schoolyard, wearily
turned in and were soon fast asleep. About midnight we woke
to the sound of angry voices outside our van. We peered around
the edge of a shade to see a crowd of young men milling around,
gesturing and arguing amongst themselves. I pulled on a pair
of jeans and sneaked out the door which locked behind me.
"Comment ca va?" I rattled off one of my few French phrases.
"How's it going?" I tried to manage a grin through my sleepy
fright. In a mixture of French, Algerian and English a skin-
headed youngster turned on me like a snarling wild animal.
"You capitalist-imperialist-exploiter have come to take over
our pure and noble Marxist country!"

He aroused his followers to attack the hundreds of mercenaries who, anyone could imagine, were lurking just inside our small converted delivery truck. In short order I unlocked the door, leapt inside, cranked the starter and prepared to flee. The diesel wouldn't so much as cough. I pulled at the control that turned on the glow-plugs and waited the required twenty seconds before cranking the starter again. In the meantime the young leader started screaming a hypnotic chant, repeating it over and over until it rose to a shriek. He was welding a group of young punks into a raging army of maniacs aflame with a holy war.

At last the engine started, and as I raced to warm it, the mob closed in. Careful not to make any jerky moves, I eased in the clutch and began to get us out of there as quickly as possible. The leader, seeing his capitalist-imperialist-exploiter escaping, ran from the open schoolyard into the narrow, fenced road followed by his band of warriors. They blocked it completely. I threw the gears into reverse and started backing down the dirt road going in the only direction open.

Megan had been directing the backwards flight and now shouted for me to stop. One of the youngsters had gone for his battered old car which wedged against our rear bumper. With threatening bodies in front and a rusty car bumping us from the rear, the situation could not have been worse.

We stayed locked in suspense, windows shut tight, engine racing. Then one of the gang went to the side of the road, picked up a loose stump and hurled it at the van. It thumped against the side with a loud bang which incited the gang who began to search the dark roadside for something to hurl. They forgot to keep the road blocked and one young man motioned for me to hurry away while the road was clear. He turned to throw a body block into one of the others who was about to step back into the road and the van surged forward leaving a cloud of dust to settle on the freedom fighters. The rusty car was too decrepit to give chase.

Shaken, we drove to a lighted service station and collapsed into a troubled sleep. The remainder of our Algerian trip passed without incident. We stopped to camp beside fantastic Roman ruins as well as in well-ordered towns; we encountered only hospitality and friendliness. Occasionally, however, we still stop to give thanks to our guardian angel and the young Algerian who threw that body block.

The Friendly Balance

People who hear our Algerian story said we ought not to camp in Moslem countries. Our experience tells us that we only chose the wrong site. We continued our travels in Tunisia and were treated everywhere as honored guests of the country, invited into homes, given presents, made welcome everywhere. We were even befriended by an old guard at the ruins of the seaport of ancient Carthage who patiently taught us the Arabic way to make tea: strong and sugared.

To avoid trouble, try to find a camping spot and get set up long before dark. Talk to someone who looks older and authoritative; tell him of your intentions and get an affirmative reaction if not outright permission. Watch your step in situations or neighborhoods that seem to threaten you, especially in places erupting with revolutionary fervor. When you fall into unsolvable or even frightening situations, pause and give the incident a chance to unfold a little more. You may easily have misread the signals; don't jump to hasty conclusions. Most incidents sort themselves out. Cultivate a peaceful, wait-and-see attitude.

Question Rumors

It's a sad situation when your destination is blocked either by actual or imagined dangers. As you travel, rumors of curious—not to mention dangerous—situations, will reach you. "Don't go THERE," somebody will say. "There are robbers, pirates, drug-crazed thieves. . . (fill in your own version of a horror story). . . . We heard from an acquaintance of a friend-of-a-friend all about it." Discount second- or third-hand stories that are not backed up with solid evidence. Question the bearer of these bad tidings and you may find that he never ventures beyond the confines of his campground or even down the street to the local market.

"You know," he or she will whisper in a frightened voice, "people at that market give me a dark look. Who knows what they are planning to do!"

We checked several such stories of dangerous situations and realized they were either distorted recountings of perfectly ordinary incidents or the projections of frightened minds. "What if. . .?" But we have also heard first-hand accounts that tell the unvarnished truth about very weird and dangerous events. Listen to and question all stories; pay attention to those people who have had real problems and find out how they intend to avoid them in the future.

A Gas Attack

Across Europe we were told not to camp for the night at a truck plaza nor beside the road anywhere near Naples. We usually don't stop in such places anyway and promptly forgot the advice. But at Amsterdam we met a couple from San Francisco who had spent the previous summer season camping along the Italian peninsula. They gave the same advice but with their first-hand account.

He was a doctor who Gypsied a couple of months each year. Their previous summer was grand. They recounted amusing incidents to us and discussed good food, superb museums and numbered the places they intended to revisit.

"But we lost our money, passports and a good many of our belongings—cameras, watches, tape deck—one night camp-

187

ing about thirty kilometers outside of Naples. We had made an extra long day of it and night caught us before we could find a proper campsite. So we pulled off the Autostrada into one of those big parking areas and stopped beside half a dozen freight trucks. The area was set well off the highway with a little forest intervening so that you could hardly hear the traffic during the night. It was peaceful and we prepared for a deep night's sleep. We got it."

Here the doctor paused, recalling everything that had happened. "It had been very hot all day so that when we went to bed we left all the windows open. You can see," and here he pointed to his van, "that all the windows are screened so we didn't have to worry about bugs. We just locked the door and went to sleep immediately."

"When we woke the sun was full up. Maud woke first feeling groggy and she had the devil of a time shaking me conscious. I came to with a colossal headache and couldn't focus my thoughts for awhile. Maud's gasp of surprise brought me around. Somebody had ransacked the place while we slept. Drawers were dumped on the floor; the closet had clothes half dragged from it. Obviously the thieves made a lot of noise, but we didn't wake. One screen had been slashed and bent back and the door was wide open. I staggered to my feet feeling like I'd been run over. It was then I noticed a lingering smell, something antiseptic, cloying and sweet. There was no doubt about it, sometime when we were hard asleep thieves shot an anesthetic gas into the camper and put us under."

The doctor knew two other couples to whom this had happened. "We understand there is an organized gang doing this and they sometimes attack truck drivers, stealing their wallets and anything else they can sell quickly. We also met a U.S. serviceman who said that the European *Stars And Stripes* advised all personnel vacationing in Italy to watch for this very same gang."

Later that year we rented a small studio in Florence and our landlady told a similar story. Fourteen of the nearby big villas had been attacked in the same way—the inhabitants gassed and kept under while antique furniture and valuable paintings were loaded onto trucks and hauled away.

This frightening bit of information had us in a quandary. Had Italy become so bandit-ridden that we would be wise to go elsewhere?

We asked the doctor what he was going to do? He told us, "I am going to continue my annual travels and camp in well-patrolled campgrounds and exercise the same precautions I would in the States. We had gotten so used to accepting the honesty of the European villagers, we forgot that big cities everywhere breed robbers."

Harbor Hurricane

On a sailboat, storms loom, rocky shores imperil and pirates lurk, yet these threats are not sufficient to dissuade enthusiasts from going to sea in small boats. Indeed thousands of private sailors take to the sea every year, but few encounter disasters. The worst storm we've experienced came while moored in Gibraltar's destroyer pens built for navy ships with stone quays twelve feet above high water. When hurricane-force winds hit, solid sheets of water crashed over these walls and brought winds so fierce we couldn't stand upright. For two days and nights we lived aboard a 38 ton boat rearing and careening at her quay like a wild horse gone berserk.

In that storm, tall steel cranes toppled over like straws in the adjacent Navy Yard and heavy equipment was bent and broken. "Greetings to your new life aboard a sail boat," seemed to be the message sent by some malevolent sea-god urging us to give up before we started. We tied multiple mooring lines to the quays as old ones snapped and rode out three days of violent seas. Then we spent days of balmy weather repairing

the damage and more such days sitting quietly in the cockpit sunning and forgetting the nightmare storm. During the quiet aftermath we planned what our boat needed to make it stronger and more capable and reviewed what we'd learned about ourselves when faced with a crisis. We delayed our trip to Spain where our recently purchased old boat was to undergo a major rebuild. The delay helped us to regain confidence in our wild venture and gave us time for better planning. To learn to make a temporary retreat is a lesson as valuable as learning when to forge ahead.

Experience Teaches

Tragedies occur when eagerness or some external force overwhelms good sense and causes us to push forward when it is better to stay put. The consequences of using poor judgement should not be blamed on unfamiliar territory; you don't have to be away from home to crack your head on a bathtub. Some acquaintances of ours let their charter clients pressure them into starting a voyage to Mallorca at the beginning of a major storm. Their fifty-foot, well-built wooden ketch sank and all hands were lost. The sea doesn't keep schedules.

Starting a trip before your craft or van has been fully checked out at a convenient and known repair agency can spell trouble when the intended route takes one to lovely, yet remote, country. You will hear plenty of sad tales about interrupted ventures— interrupted not by brigands, but by careless mechanical maintenance.

The biggest boating hazard is an untrained, inexperienced sailor who insists a sea voyage is like a day of driving on a smoothly paved road with service stations, road signs and restaurants along the way. Naivete can kill you.

"Ja. It is no more than driving my car," said my potbellied, shiny-bald, diamond-in-the-ear, thirty year old German acquaintance. Nevertheless, he begged me to help to take his newly bought second-hand boat out to the Balearic Islands. "I just thought maybe you'd know something that would help me," he pleaded. When we headed out of the well-protected port, he yelled: "Stop! Turn back! This is horrible, we can't survive in such violent seas!" The brand new sailor shook all over as the boat rocked and bucked up and down a full two inches.

He was right to be frightened, but for the wrong reasons. Lack of wind required motoring. Arriving at a nearby port, the diesel sputtered to a halt fifty feet from the dock. Lines were tossed ashore and the boat was pulled in. A mechanic came aboard to examine it. The evidence was overwhelming: this boat had lain half sunk for who knows how long, had been pumped out, and the visible half of the engine had been repainted, leaving the engine itself a rusty mess. During the time the boat had been neglected, sea water had seeped not only into the engine but into the gear box as well. Rust had destroyed them both. The new owner had bought a lemon, and at sea, a lemon sinks.

While the list of the inexperienced and careless could go on and on, no Gypsy traveler need be among them. Experience will come—you will learn quickly how to travel comfortably and well. Your best guide is an open, eager attitude that takes note of lessons and asks questions of the more experienced. Accept the humility that goes with learning new skills for a new life.

Curious events are part of every traveler's life. Whether they discourage you or are welcomed as challenges depends on your making a profound resolution to "take it all as it comes."

Avoiding Terrorism

Many people are genuinely and justifiably concerned about terrorism. It is important to remember, however, that thousands of Americans currently travel throughout the world without any trouble from terrorists. The slim possibility of terrorist attacks is given maximum media attention. Yet, the danger of having a wreck on the way to any number of U.S. airports is much, much greater. Drunken drivers on our home turf are statistically a much greater threat than international terrorists.

Terrorism is a disease of our age. Whether we like it or not, it is likely to become endemic even to North America. Should we stop traveling altogether? Fear is the true enemy to happy and fulfilled living. How you avoid and eradicate fear and begin to open up to the joy of vibrant living is the basic theme of this book and of Gypsying.

Even though the chances of your encountering terrorism are remote, there are some simple ways to practically eliminate the likelihood of finding yourself in the same neighborhood as terrorists. Remember, terrorists are seeking maximum media exposure, so:

☐ Stay away from big cities which are in the headlines.

☐ Don't use large, crowded air terminals. For example, if you must land in London, choose an airline that uses Gatwick Airport only.

☐ Do fly less publicized and less frequented routes such as Newark-Brussels.

☐ Don't use airlines that fly to or from centers of current terrorist attention.

☐ Don't attend large public spectacles, especially international competitions and fairs.

☐ Don't tempt fate by traveling into areas of maximum strife (with revolutions, mayhem, religious animosities).

☐ Keep a low profile. Don't flaunt your religion, your nationality or your money. Avoid ostentatious dress and behavior in public.

☐ Don't eat or sleep where there are hordes of North American, British or Israeli tourists or servicemen.

WHAT TO WEAR

Dress For Camping

Outfitting for Gypsying is simple: dress for comfort and hard wear. Plan just as you would for an extended camping trip and all the right decisions will follow. Since this is not to be a short holiday don't think of a "wardrobe" with this item to be worn when you visit here and that item there. Loose, soft clothing is essential. Look for materials that wash easily and colors that don't show the dirt.

We didn't know this at first. Men's chino pants looked like a winner to me but if I didn't carefully hang them up each night they were a wrinkled crush by morning. When I checked the oil level in the van a black spot stained them and it never did get out. Wash and wear sport shirts, skirts and blouses are no good either. They tear easily, cease to look fresh and neat after a month and the buttons pry loose.

Fatigues For Fun

Trial-and-error has left us with the sort of work clothing issued to sailors; dark blue for everything from socks to underwear to shirts and pants. Denim wears like iron; knit shirts and underwear are carefree.

Easy Shopping

For easy shopping, Penny's, Montgomery Ward's and L.L. Bean's sell most everything you'll need. These brands are mentioned in our appreciation for good products and services. We have no financial interest in them whatsoever.

All-Round Clothing

Jeans with a full, old-fashioned cut roll nicely for storage and can be worn on almost any occasion. Many travelers find a long sleeve cotton turtleneck the very best all-round shirt. Under a lightweight jacket it looks acceptable even in fancy establishments. Try different brands since some begin to sag after a half dozen washings and you end up with the appropriate shape for a long-armed orangutan with a very short torso. The cotton-synthetic blends hold their shape best and come in a rainbow of colors. Fuzzy dacron socks, all the same navy color, are the right weight for most climates.

Hot Weather Informality

Around campsites, on a boat or at the beach, the warmer the weather the more informal the attire. The briefest of shorts are worn by both men and women. Cut-off jeans or rugby shorts with an elastic waistband do as well. Put your bare feet in rubber flip-flops if anything at all. In really hot climates women wear halter tops while men go shirtless.

Dress-Up Occasions

A full skirt, a sleeveless top and a jacket all made of a washable pre- crushed Indian cotton give women a variety of dressing combinations. If you like original peasant clothes, take these along. A calf-length brightly embroidered cotton shift from southern Mexico can be worn in Europe, North Africa and the Middle East and considered neither formal nor informal but good looking.

We were apprehensive when we were invited out to a posh restaurant in the South of France and had only jeans to wear. But we should not have worried; movie stars, oil sheiks, playboys and playgirls wore jeans. Of course theirs were topped with silk shirts, linen jackets and glittering jewelry.

Genuine, born-in-the-wagon Gypsies teach us to add a bright printed scarf tied around our necks. A cotton bandanna in a yellow or red print, or a multicolored silk scarf from India, is as natural to my wife as high heel shoes are not; for me it took a bit of courage to wear a bandanna until I remembered all those old cowboy movies. If Tom Mix could, why not me?

For Meeting The Queen

Appropriate clothing for that veddy, veddy formal occasion is available in the big cities at rent-a-rag stores. For a price, they fit you in white tie and tails, satins, ermines and sometimes tiaras. But if you're in the Middle East or North Africa you can go into a bazaar and for a small price buy men's djalabas, women's kaftans, bedouin dresses and harem finery, and arrive at the formal occasion looking like a Khan or his Begum.

Shoes On Either Foot

All you need is one pair of perfectly fitted walking shoes. Low heeled, low quarter leather shoes, with plenty of toe space—you know the type. They should be handsome as well when a cleaning and a polishing bring them back to standards.

Important advice: wear your new shoes for a month at home to prove they are exactly the right fit. Nothing can ruin your trip more than tortured feet.

It will be easy to fill out your shoe wardrobe while you're traveling. In most countries you can purchase inexpensive canvas loafers and rubber sandals for the hot season.

Don't count on finding a good fit anywhere in southern Europe, however, because the cobbler's lasts from which they're made are an inhuman size. In England you'll find what you need, but you will pay more than in the States.

Sports Clothing

Specialized clothing such as rubber boat boots, heavy raingear—anything needed for a hunt to a scuba dive—can be purchased abroad as you need it. Many of the better brands sold in the U.S. for skiing, windsurfing and such are manufactured in Europe anyway.

Cold Weather Clothing

Since you will be living abroad during the four seasons and the weather will swing from 100 degree heat to 0 degree cold, it seems as if even a steamer trunk wouldn't hold all the clothing you'll need. Take a lesson from mountain climbers who begin the trek wearing the least amount of clothing and add layer on layer as they ascend. I carry two lightweight wool sweaters that I can wear either singly or together. For long stays in wet, cold places such as England and Scandinavia, a pair of long johns comes in handy. Silk long underwear is easy to wash and is warm and comfortable because it's not bulky.

Cat In A Hat

Unless you have a favorite old Stetson, headgear should be purchased overseas. Hats become an adventure in disguise. In southern France and Spain a soft wool beret will transform you into a local. Farther south near the Mediterranean big straw hats hide your foreign freckled face from view and the hot sun. In Tuscany the very lightweight colored straw hats distinguish you as a grape picker. In Moslem countries the men wear knitted or crocheted beanies downtown and in the country add a wrapped turban to it. Why not look like Omar the tent maker? You're here for the adventure, so be venturesome.

Emergency Clothing

In England during one of their wettest, coldest winters, our clothing was continually damp. There was nothing to do but find heavyweight wool tweeds. It was then we discovered the poor man's Saville Row: Oxfam Stores, a charity for the impoverished citizens of third-world countries. The affluent donate clothing for resale at these stores. Barely worn, good quality tweed skirts, slacks and coats line the racks. For less than ten dollars, Megan and I were both nicely outfitted. We even got wool house robes thick as army blankets. When we left England we donated our purchases back to Oxfam.

Flea markets and second-hand stores can meet wardrobe emergencies in most European cities. A first foray into one second-hand shop shocked my sensibilities. Me? Wearing who knows what kind of used clothes that had covered whom? That thought went out the window fast when I saw freshly cleaned, high-quality clothing to be had for peanuts. The savings could be applied to further travel. What is the best choice? False pride or more travel? Would you look at this Barcelino hat I'm wearing? Swell isn't it? Looks like James Cagney as a Chicago gangster! I got a double bargain when I bought it; it only cost me four dollars and the loss of a stiff neck.

Wear Washables

Avoid clothing that requires dry cleaning because it is very expensive overseas. Even good wool clothing can be washed as long as it doesn't have inner linings that stay wrinkled from the washing. Wash everything once to test it before you pack it. Of course it may be worth it to you to take one dry-clean-only item.

Invisibility

Desideratum is to dress discreetly. Most churches and hallowed places specifically require covered shoulders, arms encased above the elbows, trousers for men, skirts or slacks for women. Convention is especially offended by women who

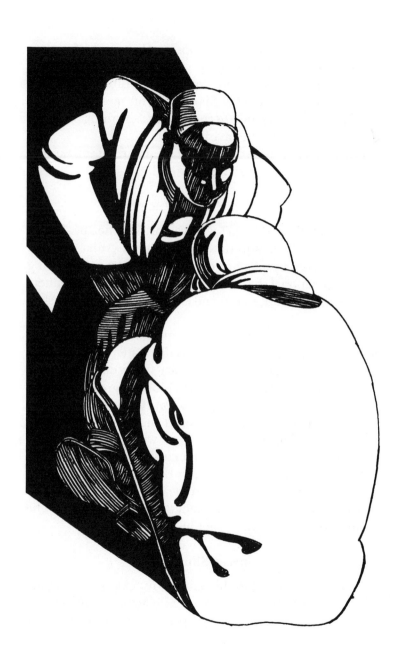

are scantily clad. Shorts, halter tops, and bare midriffs are appropriate around campgrounds or aboard boats in hot weather but they raise eyebrows and scorn from traditional cultures. On the other hand there is this bizarre "no-see-um" attitude in summer when the northerners arrive. Anything blatantly outlandish seems to be invisible.

Out of season, dress close to the local norm if you want to be welcomed and considered a friend.

A Case Of Too Much

A young American girl was staying with her boyfriend after the tourist season in southern Spain. Anita received more than the usual amount of attention from the young male population if she went shopping alone. When the attention shifted to propositions and crude suggestions, she asked for advice.

This part of Spain was old fashioned and normally young men didn't act this way. What was the matter? The obvious problem was that she displayed particularly enticing curves and a very pretty face. Indeed, she looked a great deal like a well-known movie star, and, consciously or not, dressed like her. Her skirts were way undersized and mini, her sweaters were intended for her smaller sister with one third the endowments. When she moved her curves rumba-ed and her breasts samba-ed.

Megan helped the girl cut out new blouses and skirts and sew them into conventional length full-cut clothing. The would-be toreadors no longer lunged at her.

Special Situations

There are topless beaches and nudist colonies along the Mediterranean, but these are carefully screened and fenced and far from towns. Admission is permitted only to foreigners.

At Sea

At sea, the sun and outdoor activities cause everyone to shed layers down to the bare essentials. Take care to cover up the epidermis when you leave the grounds of the clubs, marinas, beaches and other tourist areas. Be especially discreet in your manner of dress if you're in rural Greek and Spanish villages and even more so in Moslem areas. You'll see the older women still draped from head to toe in black. Their custom is to show they are married by wearing black, the color of propriety and unavailability.

A Woman's Cover-up

Megan and I have had many discussions about what a Western woman should wear in a Moslem country to camouflage her foreignness and help open the doors of the natives. Of course no foreign woman can pass altogether unnoticed, but how much better for her not to stand out too strongly in a crowd.

The Western woman is accustomed to wearing attention-getting clothing, hair-styles, makeup and jewelry. If a woman wants to reduce the amount of attention that she receives in a Moslem country, a head and shoulders shawl with an end drawn across the lower part of her face helps her blend into the background.

Luggable Luggage

Pack in soft luggage with shoulder straps for short backpacking from train to trolley, plane to bus. Once you've acquired your moving home your luggage must disappear into very small storage spaces. If it rolls into a tight bundle you've selected the right kind. Also take a small day-pack with padded straps for shopping trips into the markets or for overnight journeys away from your van or boat.

KEEPING IN TOUCH

The Absent Communication System

Keeping in touch can loom as an obstacle to going away for months or years. Keeping in touch with family, friends and world news can gain in importance with distance and remoteness.

Personal communication was so simple when we touch-dialed eleven digits and two rings later talked to our daughter-in-law about our grandson. Though she was two thousand miles away we felt as if she were in the next room. After a leisurely chat, we sat musing over our grandson's latest antics. The phone rang again, our daughter-in-law has called back: "Forgot to tell you, Iaian's just cut another tooth."

Our communications are so simple and immediate—phoning next door or to the next state, snapping on the TV to get the latest news flash, opening the promptly delivered morning paper, flipping through a stack of magazines—that we forget it is pure miracle. Now here we are venturing way beyond nowhere and keeping in touch becomes well nigh impossible.

Our first travel experience taught us that we had to find an easy way to keep in personal touch with family and friends and some simple method of receiving world news. At the same time we didn't want the means to interfere with our travel's tranquility. What to do?

A Personal Communication Service

For personal communication, we joined British Monomarks, a London-based, private mail and communications forwarding company. After paying the annual fee, a box number was assigned which became our new, personal address whenever we were to be overseas. We got a phone number for getting messages. From that time, anyone who wished to get in touch could write or call BM and be assured that we would receive their message in the shortest possible time. [See Appendix G]

As BM members we can write, call or Telex London to receive emergency messages or instruct BM where to send our next batch of mail. Let's say you are traveling in Turkey and know you'll be in Izmir in ten days time. You instruct BM to forward all accumulated mail to the central post office, c/o General Deliver, Izmir. With experience, you know that General Delivery is called Poste Restante, Fermo Posta or Lista de Correos—depending on the country. And if there is unreliable mail service within that country, BM would know to send letter-mail only and hold packages until you've arrived in a country in which valuables won't simply disappear.

The Monomark people have arranged rendezvous with family members for us in London, Ibiza, Athens and Casablanca.

International News

For world news, as well as stock market reports and good music, travelers depend on BBC World Service broadcasts. All that is required is a good short-wave radio. You can pick up or subscribe to the BBC program guide "London Calling" at a British Consulate or Information service office. It's a mighty useful guide since short-wave frequencies shift during the day and shift again as you move from one geographical area to another.

Telephone Disservice

Overseas telephone service is uneven in quality; quite often the wait for a connection runs into hours and the quality of sound is so poor you are sorry you went to the trouble. Plus, the cost can be enormous. If you travel to remote areas, be prepared to forego phoning entirely.

Don't call from hotels and "special service" offices as there is NORMALLY a surcharge of 200 to 400 percent! But you can budget in short calls from the public phone offices located in all cities. We kicked the telephone habit and returned to the fine old art of letter writing.

Telexing

When telephone connections are impossible, Telex-talk works fine. Remote outposts have their electronic typewriters for sending and receiving immediate replies—you can actually watch the paper unroll while the keys type the messages going both ways. There are public telex facilities in all cities and most large villages all over Europe and North Africa. In some, you can actually sit at the machine and do the typing yourself. In others, it's possible to hover over the operator. Sadly, Telex doesn't work so simply in the States.

International Periodicals

Popular North American news magazines publish European editions, and even an overseas edition of the Wall Street Journal is served up daily in all the major cities. Suppose you were reading an article describing the Middle Eastern situation and you've just visited a Crusader Fortress at Acre, Israel. You might develop a sense of how history repeats itself.

Writers for International editions of U.S. magazines, however, appear to lack a background in world history. Their articles are hopelessly tied to a North American viewpoint. And who needs that when one is seeing things on the spot where history was made? Writers for the London "Economist" [See Appendix B], available in most cities, have more insight.

War, destruction and disaster are part of the world's reality, but not the whole picture. Many who spend long periods abroad living close to situations of world importance are reassured to find in these crises additional faces to the news.

A published account presents but one editorial consideration. Traveling, being on the spot, gives us the opportunity to expand that viewpoint or discover several others. We find the "bad guys" are human beings like ourselves, the events multi-faceted, the desire for understanding universal.

Art Of Letters

When we began communicating by letter alone we were richly rewarded. Our faltering first postcards saying "Having a fine time, etc. . ." shifted to letters, some running to pages of descriptions, feelings and ideas. Writing forced us to review our situation, to remember and recall impressions of places and events. Rereading and editing our letters increased our enjoyment as experiences "warmed us twice."

An equal reward comes in the return mail. Family members and friends communicate truly, saying what we've longed to hear. They describe poignant scenes at home, revealing their emotions and observations. By returning to the art of the letter, we were drawn closer. By going away, by loosening the beggarly bonds of instant communication, we began to touch depths and profundities. And unlike the fugitive phone voice, the written word can be reread and savored.

The Correspondence Scene

When you receive a letter overseas it is no ordinary occurrence; often it's the high point of the day. The scene in Ibiza town is typical: on the north side of the plaza, the outside wall of the Sol Y Mar Cafe is flooded with sunshine and foreigners who gather here after picking up their morning mail at the Post Office. They sink into chairs set about tiny tables, order coffee, plunge into personal letters, or scan magazines or papers bought at the nearby kiosk. For a time the only sounds come from the crackling of paper and the sipping of coffee, followed by sighs, exclamations or "humphs." Heads turn to see who else is around. Greetings are exchanged and talk begins.

Truer Communications

Gypsying doesn't cut you off from essential communication with family or friends or information. It does allow you to eliminate useless or shallow exchanges. It's hard to realize until you're actually on the road, how much time has been stolen by the media and jabbering telephones. Travel provides an opportunity to take a longer view of current events and get a deeper insight into relationships. You're seemingly cut off, yet you're actually closer to history in the making and the essence of people.

BATHING AND STAYING CLEAN

Bathing

We Gypsies aren't the John Bunyan type, overly hearty, smelling of wood smoke and sweat. We may be casual, but we're always clean.

"But how do you bathe?" queried our fastidious friend who was staying at a deluxe hotel and visiting our simple camper. What, she wondered, did we do without a tiled bathroom equipped with shower and tub?

F. P. C. Technique

Hoping our B.O. wasn't overpowering, we explained the process used by experienced travelers faced with a shortage of water and a deficit of plumbing. Spirited wayfarers take an F.P.C. bath, the European method of staying clean. Positively recommended. Quick, utilizing the least amount of water, F.P.C. is a morning and night routine that leaves us refreshed . . . and generally shiny.

For F.P.C. heat a saucepan of water, pour this into a wash basin or small sink and dunk in a sponge, a washcloth or loufa scrubber and you're set. Wet the face, apply soap followed by scrubbing and rinsing. Proceed to the next area: the arm pits and back of the neck. Repeat the washing and rinsing process and proceed to the next area: to the lower, middle part of the anatomy. Try this sometime standing on a towel and you can transform any warm spot into a bathing room.

Physiologists explain that where one perspires the most requires washing the most. Wash in these three vital areas (F.P.C.), and you will feel clean and refreshed. Once you adopt the F.P.C. routine, a tub bath or shower shifts from necessity to luxury.

With a simple way to get clean, your perspective changes

concerning van and boat choices. No longer will you demand the big space-wasters of complete bathing rooms—especially those with built-in tubs. You'll find almost any private spot will do for a clean-up so long as it is free from drafts and confines the scatter of water.

Shampooing

Shampooing is a different matter. Unless he's nearly bald, a man needs a full bucket of warm water, women require two.

Depending on season and weather, most people find they don't absolutely need to shampoo more than twice a week. Most women try to simplify their needs by having a very short hairstyle. Others let their hair grow long and tie it up so that they do not need permanents and other special treatments. Though longer hair requires more washing and drying time, those silken tresses easily form into pigtails, or top knots that always look well-groomed. Add a hair clip, a bit of ribbon, a flower and you have an old fashioned but convenient and mighty handsome coiffure.

Special Experiences

It's fun remembering the circumstances and places we've had our F.P.C.'s. Once we stayed in a whitewashed cell in a pension in a Moroccan village—a white floor, white walls and even a white ceiling. A tiny window let in a wedge of light and a puff of air. Down the hall a wash basin yielded icy water. This was the only accommodation in that village, but it gave us the chance to meet Moroccans. The sparse cell told of their ordinary housing and the custom of whitewashing to brighten and clean living spaces. From our backpack we took a little saucepan, filled it and returned to our room. Lighting a single-burner camp stove fitted to a pint-sized bottle of butane, we proceeded to heat the water and moved into our

F.P.C. routine. We felt clean after a dusty trip.

We recall F.P.C.'s in Venice, near an Orthodox monastery in Yugoslavia, in the hinterlands of Israel and Turkey and beside a Scottish Loch. Quick cleansing leaves us lots of time for more adventures.

The Necessary Big Bath

After a series of F.P.C.'s we are more than ready for the BIG BATH. Indeed life, in all its fullness, demands the BIG BATH.

The BIG BATH is not vital maintenance, it is pure hedonism. Searching, scouting, angling for the BIG BATH is almost as much fun as taking it. In Gibraltar, rumor had it that there was a public bath house with jumbo sized tub baths. Our search began immediately. After stumbling into a mysterious hotel that refused to rent a room to anybody, then bumbling into what turned out to be an automobile agency with no cars for sale, we asked a man on the street. He directed us down an alley between two buildings where we were to "veer left." We "veered," almost fell off the sea wall, found what looked like the city jail but turned out to be the very welcome bath house.

A bath attendant led us into a private room where we found a lordly bath tub wide as a bed. We watched as, muttering and grunting, he turned on taps which were the size of fire hydrants. Next, he demanded we test the water. When we shrieked from the scalding, he put the faucet key in his pocket and withdrew satisfied. But oh, when we finally slid down into that hot, hot water and sank right up to our noses and then lingered, soaking in the heat, we entered a realm of ecstasy not available to those who take bathing for granted.

Bath With Beans

On the island of Rhodes in the heart of the old Medieval quarters, moss clings to stone walls that have been splashed with Crusaders' blood. Amidst the ancient stones we found a famous pension much beloved by young people from all parts of the globe. For a hot water bath we had to burn a bundle of twigs at the bottom of a tall copper heater and wait thirty minutes until the geyser erupted.

The kitchen was communal and contained the bath tub. After a week passed, we grew tired of bathing while cooks stirred the beans. We wanted something different. Fortunately Rhodes is graced with a sensational sensuous solution!

The Great Turkish Bath

We found a multi-domed Hammam on a nearby plaza. Despite having been built by the hated Turks some centuries before, this fantastic bath house was maintained perfectly.

At the modest entrance we exchanged money for a brass tag and a couple of threadbare but clean towels. Inside, a vast dome, theatrical as a mosque, rose above a square room with daylight shooting through the star-shaped holes in the ceiling. These sent lancets of brilliance to a marble floor. We went to separate men's and women's portions to enter regions of Arabian Nights delight.

On two sides of a big room, wooden platforms rose three feet to support latticed-screened dressing cubicles. Undressed and draped with a towel, I stepped down and headed for a door at the far end of the room. The floor of big polished marble slabs was surprisingly warm. On the other side of the door the warmth rose to a tropical jungle heat. Beyond it I entered a domed bathing room from which Moorish arched doorways beckoned towards other domed spaces.

Moving deeper into the place, the roof lowered and the heat grew fierce since, under the floors, flames coursed through a hollow space. I dipped cool water from a marble basin, sluiced myself clean and lingered to absorb more heat.

Finally I imitated other bathers by laying on the smooth

marble floor to look up at the motes of mist playing in the slender shafts of light and to dream of perfumed gardens in an Islamic paradise attended by Houris. A beautiful languorousness stole over me, consciousness began to drift.

It took a long, long time to come back and face the world. I dragged myself to a cooler room to allow the sweating to stop and to sluice once again. I wondered if I had the will-power even to push open the door to the dressing room. I might just stay here forever in this rapture of warmth and domed light.

Eventually I dressed and departed. Over the years we've returned there and to other Hammams across North Africa and Turkey to reclaim the world of the BIG BIG BATH and . . . ecstasy.

Creating Your Own BIG BATH

When the weather is warm the BIG BATH calls you out-of-doors. One spring we camped beside a ruined farmhouse on Ibiza island. Three walls and part of the roof remained, and the gaping hole where the fourth wall once stood overlooked a field swaying with yellow daisies. During the day sun poured into that opening, warming the stone walls. Here two full buckets of warm water, a sponge and a dipper gave the luxury of a BIG BATH in puris naturalibus.

In our van we carry a two-person standup tent. When we stop for longer than a day or two, up goes the tent for that extra room that serves as a study, day lounge, and, when the sun has heated the space, a warm bathing room.

A full bath requires heating quantities of water and this in turn demands ingenuity. You can always employ your cook stove to do that job but the long hours of summer sunshine can take its place. Camping stores stock solar showers—black plastic bladders with a shower head at the bottom. Suspend this gadget filled with water from the branch of a tree, wait for the sun to heat it, open the valve and step under.

Or a dark brown plastic dish pan filled with water and set in the sun does just about as well. When the wind blows, stretch a layer of clear plastic over the top to trap all the sun's heat and prevent wind cooling.

Or A Mini-Bath

When the BIG BATH is not attainable, travelers accept a mini-BIG BATH as substitute. Not a tank, not a tub, the mini is merely a shower. You can nearly always find showering facilities near slipways used by fishing boats. Along German and Dutch main highways there are strategically located restaurants catering to truckers and there you'll find showers too. Enjoy an excellent meal and the cost of the showers is thrown in. The larger service stations on the German Autobahns have unmarked showers for truckers that you're usually welcome to use.

Ferryboats often provide showers for deck passengers who don't take a cabin. If they seem to be hidden away, talk to a friendly truck driver making the same trip, and he'll lead you to all that flowing hot water. Indeed, truckers on land or on sea usually know where the showers and good restaurants are.

When all else fails, head for a campground with advertised showers. A camping guide may list the hot water, but does a particular camp have a functioning water heating system? Better walk in to check with resident campers first. You'd be amazed how many places go on, year after year, having "temporary" shutdowns for repairs.

Spa Bathing

Mineral springs are a good substitute if neither BIG BATH nor mini is available. Europeans take their spas seriously and erect hospitals and hotels around them. At such an establishment you must use persuasion to get a bath only and not a treatment.

In northern Portugal, we soaked up healing waters in pink marble sunken tubs while medical attendants in white coats hovered as we protested we wanted only to get clean.

South of Florence at the Baths of Saturn there is a surplus of hot water from the spa. This excess flows a half mile through a deep ditch and flings itself over a cliff to form a steaming waterfall. Below these falls the minerals have molded pools and dips and natural tubs. Two hours soaking in this sulphur water while gazing out across a flower filled valley lifted our spirits to Gypsy heights.

Friendly Offers

When you stay in one spot for awhile English-speaking people, curious about your casual life, will come for a visit and stay for a drink or a meal. After inspecting your van they usually see that a bath with plenty of hot water at their house would be the best way for them to return your hospitality. You'll soon have a circuit of friends from England to Italy who will invite you for a visit and a bath.

Laundry Facilities

Bathing stimulates the desire for clean clothes and this leads, sad to say, to laundry. Campgrounds furnish water: the first requirement. Sometimes they provide washing machines. More often they provide scrub tubs. In any case, experienced travelers have a collection of washing buckets.

Some campgrounds supply such strange built-in wash tubs that you grow to appreciate your simple buckets. Campground wash tubs at Coimbra, Portugal are cast in concrete to a depth and width that arches the body into a backbreaking posture. Worse than this are their pedestaled scrub boards chiseled from rough grey granite. One scrub and your clothes are shredded.

Laundry Simplified

Laundry is easier with simple wardrobe and bedding. . . all in a solid dark color. Roughing it can be ruined if you're trying to keep white things spotless.

England has laundromats where you can do your own laundry. But all through northern Europe you must leave it for an attendant to do.

In Greece, Italy and North Africa laundromats are few and far between. The rare machine laundry looks like a fancy boutique with prices to match. You can figure that just over a couple of washings in one such place equals the cost of your wardrobe.

Strong Soaps

The detergents familiar to us in the States have been reformulated for use around the Mediterranean into a much stronger version expressly compounded for cold water washing. They also contain overly strong bleaching agents. We learned to use half the recommended amount.

In Spain be cautious about leaving clothes with attendants. Invariably they use too much detergent and dump in a pint of chlorine for good measure. A new pair of jeans turns baby blue on the first washing and falls apart on the third.

Sailor's Solution

When laundry problems threaten to overtake your well planned travels, try the "Sailor's Solution." We had a great demonstration of this when visiting aboard a very large, very luxurious three-masted German sailing yacht. On the deck, a dignified, retired U-boat captain was busily doing his laundry. He stood erect at the railing, grasped the sawed-off handle of a plumber's plunger, and sloshed it up and down in a plastic bucket full of soapy water. He tossed in a few articles of clothing, pumped five or six times then exchanged those clothes for another bunch. At the end of this cycle he shifted to rinse water running each article of clothing through it twice.

The plunger's motion duplicates the action of an automatic washing machine. The proof of its successful function came with his sparkling white Captain's uniforms.

"The trick," he said, "is to make each person responsible for his own laundry; he tends not to wear so many clothes." Doing your own personal washing and not asking anyone else for help cuts down on the number of clothes you change into for the sake of fashion. With a small wardrobe and a medium-sized bucket it's easier to do frequent small washings instead of waiting for the all-at-once laundry day.

Purified In Portugal

We had a large mound of dirty linen when we rolled into the ancient and charming town of Chaves, Portugal. We proposed to spend time in worthwhile sightseeing and to get the laundry done commercially. Everything in Portugal was so inexpensive that we figured laundromats would be too. At one shop clearly marked "laundry" I was told that everybody did theirs at home and this place only accepted dry cleaning. "But, on the other hand," said the proprietor, "my wife isn't busy. She'll take them home and you can pick them up in two days."

The next day, crossing the old Roman bridge over the darkly polluted river that abutted our campground, I looked down with horror at a woman kneeling beside the river slapping my slacks against the rocks. The sight was too awful to share with my wife. On the third day, I picked up our clothes. . . "clean and fresh."

PLUMBING ARRANGEMENTS

A Room Without

When you leave North America, leave your expectations for high-tech plumbing at home. Across the Atlantic good plumbing is a luxury, not a necessity. It is arranged according to different priorities.

In the small Northern European hotels, each room is equipped with a hand-washing basin and little else. To find more complicated facilities such as toilets, tubs or showers you have to petition the hotel clerk. He'll issue you a separate key and give you directions for finding these plumbing compartments down the hall.

Although newer, more expensive hotels are changing this pattern, the private bathroom is still the exception. For a high tariff you can always go to a five-star establishment and get what you want without further ado. Many Americans recoil in horror when they are offered something less than the full fixture combination. Hoteliers who have caught on, tell these customers there are no vacancies, when actually, there are plenty of vacant rooms available but without baths.

The Gypsy lifestyle requires a tightened budget and revised plumbing standards. Try out the room-with-basin. We did and found it didn't matter as much as we thought.

Expect Something Different

In Europe it's important to recognize which fixtures should do what. You may think you're familiar with a piece of porcelain only to find out you were very wrong.

We avoided a certain piece of porcelain through sheer ignorance. We thought perhaps that very low thing hiding behind a screen was a hand-washing basin for tiny tots. At a friend's party this fixture held crushed ice and bottles of champagne.

"Ah ha," I thought. "So that's it."

I started to thank the host for enlightening me.

His startled look stopped me. "That's only one use for a bidet!" he laughed.

Expect The Historic

When traveling into new regions don't flee in disgust over the plumbing. Some of the most exciting cities and towns we visit were built hundreds of years ago when what we now know as plumbing simply wasn't around. We have to recall that about 400 A.D. the Roman Empire fell and with it those brilliant Roman engineers disappeared along with the art of plumbing. Its rediscovery took hundreds of years.

Scents Of Athens

Navy friends of ours moved into family quarters built for the sixth fleet and were dunked straight into the Athens plumbing problem. The lobby of the elegant highrise is impressive with its huge sheets of plate glass, glistening marble walls and floors. Swiftly, a hushed elevator transports us to the ninth floor where the softly lit, carpeted hallway leads us to their apartment. By golly, the ol' navy sure sets up its folk right. However, something stinks.

Everyone knows that Athens is a very ancient city and so expects to overlook certain things. Yet this apartment building is new. What's making that smell? The bathroom has marble floors, ceiling-high ceramic tile, pale tan fixtures that gleam and sparkle. Yet the drain holes in both the huge shower and the wash basin are stuffed with cloth. And the window stands wide open despite the freezing air.

In the heavily draped living room of our friends, long-time residents, we asked, "What's wrong!"

"Oh," came the reply. "Just Greek plumbing."

Although the water arrived at faucets (part of the time) and drain pipes weren't broken or stopped up (mostly) and the fixtures were the best available, Greek plumbers didn't seem to understand the principle of trapping and venting sewer gases. All outlets had to be stoppered shut when they were not in use, or else the gaseous odors leaked over the air conditioned splendor.

The Squatter

Eastward to Greece, Yugoslavia, Turkey and beyond we encountered another fixture that's as mysterious as its oriental origins.

On a Greek ferryboat I sought the public conveniences. An arrow pointed the way: W.C. Stepping down three deck levels, I found it, went in, immediately backed out and rushed upward to find the ship's steward. We returned down the three deck levels, to the steel bulkheaded room. I opened a private cubicle and pointed: "How do you use that thing?"

Inside, the floor was sculpted with a porcelain pan looking like a misshapen shower. Towards the back a hole yawned, and two islands rose from the sides shaped like giant foot prints. When you pushed a handle down on the wall, water whooshed from a pipe sending out a cascade that flushed the thing and spilled out onto the floor as well. But where was the W.C.?

The knowledgeable steward indicated, in pantomime, how to employ the twisted floor. One reversed, backed in, and with his feet set above flood level on the two islands, squatted. At this point the ship's horn gave a loud blast and I rushed up to the main, sunny deck to see what was going on, and thus avoided other things.

Eventually I learned to use the squatter. Many declare it a more comfortable and potentially more hygienic device than the W.C. of our conventional experience. But even the most modern examples don't seem to adequately control the flushing mechanism since they produce an exuberance of water that flows and flows until it threatens to flood (and sometimes does) the surrounding floor.

And Farther East

You learn, sooner or later, the "Law of the Eastward Trek": THE NEARER THE EAST, THE NASTIER THE NECESSARIES. Journeying ever eastward the plumbing changes demonically. It's been contrived with less and less concern for function or sanitation. When you arrive at the great city of Istanbul, even before finding a hotel, drag yourself to the Grand Bazaar (all forty acres of it). Look for a stall that sells rain gear and you'll find squatter-users' paraphernalia: galoshes tall enough to reach completely over your ankles. Now you are ready to enter most Turkish restrooms. Not all. To be prepared for all of them... buy hipboots.

Changing Attitudes

Only experienced travelers realize how richly North America has been blessed with abundant, perfectly operating plumbing. We shifted from bathing leisurely to rinsing quickly when the water was frigid and the room arctic. This gives us extra time for sightseeing because we go out in the world instead of lingering in the bathroom.

Traveling in warmer regions of plumbing-less countries we use bushes or walk around to the far side of a friendly wall in lieu of braving the more pungent intimacies of badly-lit, badly-cleaned bogs. The Gypsying traveler adapts; he doesn't give up. He devises sanitary solutions to squalid situations and cleans up after himself.

Take It With You

A minimum requirement for any van is a portable chemical toilet. This piece of equipment encourages camping beyond campgrounds. Portable johns also encourage travel to exotic towns whose ancient stones entice us ever deeper into their labyrinths. You won't have to put up with their archaic, though undoubtedly historic, public conveniences.

The minimum equipment for journeying into remote parts is a handy roll of TP tucked into a purse or, at least, a wad stuffed discreetly into a pocket. Paper is not provided in restrooms. In villages, you'll discover one or two rolls, covered with dust, lying high on a top shelf behind the counter, well-guarded by shopkeepers.

Don't be overjoyed with this discovery until you have tried it. One common type sold in Greece is manufactured from rough crepe paper: the perfect barnacle remover for boat hulls. The wrapper is convincingly decorated with the picture of an elephant. Another type—perhaps it is designed for reuse—is discovered in Spain. This TP is cut from rolls of waxed paper.

For these fantastic papers, the charge for one roll is 1000 pesetas, drachmas, escudos or whatever the local equivalency. In the same village, for the same price, you can stay in a good hotel and enjoy an eight-course dinner.

Bus Warning

Planning a trip by bus into the hinterlands of some Greek island or way off into the plains of Turkey requires plenty of plumbing forethought: reduce your liquid intake before departure.

Life Without T.P.

Approaching the exotic and mysterious Middle East all evidence of TP vanishes. Thereabouts, TP is replaced by. . . ah, other arrangements. For didn't the sacred writings decree that cleanliness is next to holiness? And isn't paper and its uses unclean?

In the more elegant W.C.s, such as the bathing suites in a sultan's palace, a bidet awaits you beside the W.C., furnished with gold-plated faucets and perfumed soap. Draped on gold plated bars lie thick, fluffy towels. "Wash," is clearly implied.

In the ordinary W.C., the squatter is equipped with a separate faucet at the back and, of course, on the left hand side. At meals only the right hand rises above the table to touch the food. Etiquette requires that the contaminated left hand remain below the table top.

Going Drains

In Casablanca, we met a charming English lady who was staying in a camper next to ours. She urged us to go south and stay at Agadir, a Moroccan city squeezed between the Atlantic and the desert. She described the lush tropical plants which shade the Agadir campground. She told of the facilities, hot water and so on—it had everything.

The next day we stopped to say goodbye and thank the Englishwoman for telling us about the incredible campground.

"How nice," she beamed, "I'm sure you'll enjoy it."

As we headed off she put her finger to her lips, obviously thinking about a last minute piece of advice. Then, "Oh, by the way, I should have mentioned. The drains have gone." We nodded and left.

"What did she mean when she said "the drains have gone?" Do you suppose she was referring to Alfred and Gwen Drayne, friends from England?"

"I don't know," Megan mused. "Perhaps we heard wrong. Maybe she was saying 'cranes'. They winter down South. Maybe we won't get to see them this year."

As we pulled into the Agadir campsite, we saw the Englishwoman's promise amply confirmed. The gateway was ablaze with flowering shrubs and the driveway beckoned into cool, shaded places. A tropical Eden. After registering we walked past the office to find a suitable spot for the van. All at once the perfumed garden gave off an even wilder smell: tropical sewage. Thinking this must be some kind of mistake, we turned down a road towards the shower block and the smell increased to a nose cringing stink. All the modern facilities were set around a plumbing system that didn't function.

When an Englishman speaks of improperly handled sewage he says: "the drains have gone." It doesn't refer either to flown birds or friends.

Travel Contrasts

Gypsying is full of contrasts, and plumbing encompasses things both dreaded and delightful. Do take a chance—and expect the wonderful. By taking certain precautions—and extra TP—the Gypsy Way beckons with the promise of adventure even when the drains have gone.

STOPPING AWHILE

Prescription For Sagging Spirits

When some spot looks just too good, when some village speaks alluringly of the delights of home, of staying put to harvest impressions, it is time to stop and try it out. It needn't be costly; certainly there's no thought of buying property and settling down since the settling mood won't last that long. Take this mood for what it is— the nesting instinct getting the upper hand.

Time For Discoveries

Stopping awhile in a remote spot presents plenty of opportunities for a very busy life. A far-off rural community or a small island can offer you a number of possibilities. From our first foreign house in Greece,we delved into history and archeology. Stark and powerful ruins dating from ancient Greece, Roman, Crusader and Turkish occupations invited exploration. Even a 20th century Italian protectorate and a WW II German occupation had left distinctive detritus. Here we also sampled contemporary Greece with its island-centered culture, its fishing industry and its tourist trade. To learn and experience the feel of all this, stopping awhile is essential. With an extended residency you imitate the ancient invaders, conquerors and builders who came in centuries past; in a small way you contribute to its history. You remain outsiders since this isn't your native land, yet the long-term stay opens the door to friendships, helps you join community work and celebrations, and in this way breaks down some of the barriers between you and the host culture.

Extending Your Gypsy Quarters

The small spaces of boat and van finally cramped our style.

In the summer we had an easy solution: we spread our living outdoors. We lay on the shore or spread a blanket under the trees. But one winter we headed south until the temperature began to rise, the sun shone and flowers bloomed along the roadside. Then we started looking for a suitable house. We found what we were looking for a hundred miles south of Casablanca, on the Atlantic shore of Morocco near the little jewel city of Essouira. Eight kilometers out of town stood a typical rural house built around an inner, hidden patio. The walls kept off chilly January winds and the patio acted as a sun trap.

Go For The Dream House

When you stop awhile there will be ordinary housing available such as apartments built for tourists. Yet here is the chance to discover something entirely different from your previous experiences. Without too much trouble you can often find something exotic for your foreign home, a place that will furnish you with unusual experiences.

Before you start looking, sit still awhile to ruminate. Dream dreams, imagine possibilities, create mind castles and don't accept any old accommodation. Go on, let your imaginings run riot. What's it going to be? A cottage—thatched roof, peat fires, flowers at the door? An artist's studio overlooking the Seine? A fabulous stone castle? Want to locate along a narrow street in a Medieval village? Or a mountaintop with views of the Alps? Or a canal-side cottage with boats passing closely by your window?

Be warned that what you wish for strongly, what you picture and let the mind's eye embellish, will generate its own energy. Pretty soon, you will be taken directly to that place as it actually exists and be offered your fantasy dwelling. You have put up with a lifetime of what was practical or what was possible. Now it is time to reach out for. . .the improbable.

Finding The Spot

Listen to your inner voice, follow its promptings, act upon urges that say: "Ask here" or "Knock at that door." Now is the time to try this method of finding your foreign home. Do not be surprised when your inner voice furnishes accurate directions to the ideal room, apartment or house; this is simply part of the change Gypsying brings.

It's hard to believe entirely coincidental events led us to the island of Cos from Athens. And coincidence didn't take us to our first foreign house in a countryside as lovely as any Eden. We followed an inner guide and wandered around the lushest part of this Greek Island: among orchards and vineyards, fields and streams intermingled in a rich patchwork. There we found small whitewashed stone cottages whose garden walls provided privacy from the donkey track. We were invited into some of them, to sit in the shade of vine-covered terraces, to drink wine, to sample dried figs, to enjoy the famous welcome that Greeks give all strangers. Seeing those houses decided us right then and there this was where we were supposed to be.

Any stranger wandering around in a peasant community attracts notice immediately; a stranger who is also a foreigner sets off alarm. Our presence on a back road brought a husky farmer out of a house who knew "a leetle Engleesh."

When he learned what we wanted he said, "Come, come," and led the way down a stony track through fields heavy with crop, past isolated farm houses, and stopped in front of a house attached to a stone barn. "You like?" he asked.

Imagine a two story, stone building with a red tile roof standing back from the road behind a low wall. A graceful masonry stairway led to the upper floor with a double doorway painted bright Greek blue. Beyond the house ran one field of ripening grapes and a second field of glistening, fat red tomatoes. Paying a ridiculously low sum, we moved in and changed from travelers to dwellers.

This gave us access to the traditional way of life on Cos.

Experience Simplicity

Following that first house in a foreign country, we later had the opportunity to sample many more, all different, all arranged and equipped (unequipped) like nothing we had encountered at home. We exchanged electric lighting for oil lamps, traded indoor plumbing for a path and privy, refrigerator for screened box, cooking stove for single-burner kerosene primus. We learned to shift priorities from urban demands to rural, local availability and thereby gained the capacity and freedom to stop awhile anywhere.

Lamp lighting sent us off early to bed. Lack of heating saw us bundling up close together. With no refrigeration, daily we shopped for food, bought fresh baked bread. And all these enforced simplicities taught us to eat like the locals. In Greece it was goat cheese, olives, bread and wine, fermented on the premises. For desserts it was dried figs and raisins. And we adopted other native customs: bathing in the sea and growing close and affectionate towards a sustaining land.

Furnishings

Since a van contains everything for a complete household, you can rent an empty place, just walls and roof, and move in without buying anything except food. By shifting mattresses, bedding, linens, dishes, pots and pans, and tableware, and putting all these things into the rented space, you capture it for your own. Yet the expanded space swallows up the few things that the smaller furnished; here is the occasion to buy something local, something cheap but colorful that creates a setting of distinction.

In Greece we bought local pottery and richly colored handwoven bed covers. Years later, in Morocco, we expanded our purchases to make over the empty rooms into lushly furnished Arabic rooms. We found old, faded flat-woven tent rugs that were handsome and inexpensive. We purchased worn brass trays from a shopkeeper who considered them junk metal. Resting on foot-high blocks they served as tables. To complete the scene Megan covered our pillows with wildly colored cloth. We stored dates, fruits and almonds and started to live like Bedouins.

You wouldn't suspect there would be trouble with living without chairs and getting down to sit on those rugs; we thought anybody could do that. Just wait until you try to imitate the Bedouins' easy posture—back upright, legs tucked neatly under, folded out of the way and supporting the body. You will see market vendors sitting like that for hours at a time, men that look a hundred years old. Surely no difficulty to that.

The first time I tried the Bedouin posture I went to bed with my arms, back and legs in horrible agony. I thought about those old, old men in the market sitting on crossed legs so easily. They had been talking to beat the band, leaning way out to pick up a tea glass, laughing at jokes and not shifting their legs at all. They appeared as comfortable as could be. But then you wonder, has anyone stayed till the end of the day to watch them stand up and walk out? Could it be their hefty grandsons come by and carry them home while they are still folded up?

Different Entertainments

Whenever we live in a rural house there are few citified entertainments, so we are drawn into the lives of local people: we help with the harvests and join in their traditional celebrations. That first time in Greece we were astounded to learn "Open Sesame" originated as farmer's phrase, when we helped shake sesame seeds from the slowly opened, dried pods.

The high point of those traditional activities came with the grape crushing. One afternoon we heard a braying and a clatter like an army of devils invading. Down the track came a convoy of donkeys loaded with grapes in willow panniers. Shouting and urging them on was a buxom woman and her two shy but equally buxom daughters.

"Kalimera," the woman said in greeting, displaying a mouth of gold. She stopped the donkeys and all three began to unload the panniers, dumping the grapes into a stone vat built into our front courtyard. Within a short time the vat was full to the top with purple grapes and the young daughters slipped off their shoes, hoisted their skirts above the knees and began to trample. Occasionally, the girls sent a blushing glance in our direction. As the crushing continued, the mother dumped additional grapes around the girls' legs, the sun rose higher, the girls began to sweat and their bodies turned red from the effort and the color of the grapes. The sucking and squishing noises, the movement, the sweating bodies were too lusty an activity to be reserved for virgins.

A donkey called in the distance and one of the animals waiting in the courtyard brayed a reply. More loaded beasts approached, this time driven by the father of the house—a Greek Orthodox priest wearing full robes, albeit his working ones, stained and patched. He unloaded panniers and dumped additional grapes into the vat, sinking his daughters even deeper into their font of purple juices. He placed a clay jug under the spout at the vat; pulled a wooden plug and watched a thick stream of vital juices sluice into the vessel. Another was set under and then another and another. A year's crop had developed, swollen, come to pregnant fullness, been trampled and given birth to this harvest which now was blessed by a priest. When it had sat in darkness, fermenting, it augured well for a lusty spawn.

The girls, completely spent, pushed themselves out of the

vat. The priest bustled about scooping the grape hulls out of the vat with a rake, and dumped the mess into the empty panniers to be carried back to his fields to fertilize next year's crop. The woman gently lifted the heavy, fat jars into other panniers as carefully as if she were putting a baby to bed. With a whack to the donkeys' rumps, the family left. The girls trailed behind.

Seasons Impose Shifts

The experiences of that first house-away brought us closer to the shift of seasons and the discipline they impose. As the year turned and late fall came in gusts of cold wind shaking leaves from the trees, families in nearby houses harvested the crops, packed their belongings and started the migration back to their permanent homes high in the mountain villages. Donkeys stood patiently while trunks and boxes of household paraphernalia were lashed to their backs. Soft bales of bedding and clothing went on top. Table legs were removed, chairs were nested together and a small truck appeared to collect the bulkier items. At last all was made ready and the trek began along a road that sloped steeply upward. With the children walking along beside, the old men and women riding, with strings of goats, crates of chickens, bundles of brilliantly striped homespun blankets heaped high, no Gypsy caravan could compete in color or noise.

Cold Comfort

The tourist brochures do not give the slightest amount of information on Mediterranean winters. Remember those sun-drenched posters? And those almost nude women baking in the heat? Watch as those posters pasted to walls dampen, soak, loosen and finally slither down the walls, turn into pulp, disintegrate into slush and wash down flooded streets.

What happened to the posters almost happened to us, and we had to abandon our rural idyll for the drier spaces of a nearby small city. When the constant rain arrived, we rented the upstairs apartment owned by our landlady and moved into what promised to be relative comfort. Or so we thought. We were shocked whenever it rained to watch water pour in around the window frames and at having to light candles when the town's generating plant often flooded. Dampness darkened the inside of the walls and a green mold began to grow profusely where snails appeared to harvest this luxuriant crop. When their nibbling kept us awake at night, we reconsidered the winter season in . . . the "sunny" Mediterranean.

Generally, however, in winter the Mediterranean is your best bet for stopping awhile. Latitude 35° runs across the center, so move slightly south of it when winter's grip is hardest. But pockets of warmth and sunshine can be found north of it due to the high mountains that protect some coastal plains. The Algarve in Portugal, the Almeria area in Spain, the southern coast of Crete and Turkey (facing Cyprus) are fine when Europe is not inundated with rain. But if a terrible winter hits, you can go to Israel or North Africa. The coast near Agadir in Morocco is sunny as is Marrakech and Essouira. The Tunisian town of Karouian, at the edge of the Sahara, is bright and warm.

About three out of every four summers in central Europe is sweltering. Then Ireland, Scotland and the Brittany peninsula of France are enticing. The Pyrenees mountains, which form the border between France and Spain, are high and cool, as are the Alps that reach through Austria, Switzerland, Italy and France. [See Appendix C]

Learning From Stopping Awhile

The whole story of that first "stopping awhile" became a useful lesson since it included many, many pluses and a few minuses. We checked climate in advance from people who had actually lived there. We moved when the situation no longer pleased us.

Rental Opportunities

It's not too difficult, out of season, to find a place to rent. The tourists leave, houses go empty, rental costs drop. On the Spanish island of Ibiza, as in many other locations, rental agents manage vacation houses owned by Germans and Scandinavians. There are also remotely located, temporarily empty houses, watched over by a caretaker; find him and strike a deal. You run into English entrepreneurs who have lists of apartments held specifically for tourist rental—in season or out. In Greece, in Italy, Malta, on mainland Spain and on adjacent islands, you'll find plenty of places specifically built for the short stay tourist. In season they will be expensive; out of season dickering is possible and expected.

If rental agents list places too expensive or too dull, ask at second-hand bookstores run by English-speaking expatriates or a bar that caters to the local foreign colony. Look for notice boards which list rental opportunities. Where the city is big enough to support consulates, the American, British or Canadian ones usually keep housing lists. Advertised flats are often expensive and suitable for vacationing millionaires. But this is nonetheless a worthwhile service to be looked into. As you pursue their directions you may pass empty rooms or perfectly fine unused servants quarters that the consulate thought unworthy of mention. You won't be interested in most of the offerings made to student groups, yet they do tend to connect up with local networks not available to older people. Within those networks there are perfect houses. Youth hostels in all countries, except Bavaria, allow oldies, too, as long as we don't displace card-carrying young members for whom they are being run. Hostels are located in the center of activities in all cities. On Crete one winter, we lived as hostlers and met some great young people.

Special Residences

Residential Hotels are apartments complete with private baths and kitchens with hotel service. These are always expensive but much less so than staying at an ordinary hotel and eating at restaurants. Usually less conveniently located, often far out in the country, certain monasteries offer very simple accommodations for travelers. They offer shelter for those trudging on pilgrimage. In Portugal and Spain these monasteries lie along a path which connects important shrines.

Grapevine Want Ads

Unlike a tourist, a Gypsy is never in a hurry. Finding a place for stopping awhile can be done at your leisure, so be choosy. Take time to hang around the center of community activity, such as the friendly bar. Strike up an acquaintance with the proprietor—let him put the word out to everybody about what you want. Remember that the drinking place (taverna, kafeneon, bodega, pub, etc.) is the Europeans' place for social contact and quasi-office, real estate included. In the Middle East and North Africa it is the only place for such delicate negotiations. In a tea house, you could be fortunate enough to make contact with a man who has a cousin, who knows a woman, who. . .and in the course of events move in to an unadvertised bargain. That's how we finally rented our Moroccan menage.

Avoiding Tourist Crush

During the heavy tourist season, escape to remote villages where life revolves in centuries-old patterns. We found one high in the mountains of Crete. Despite the inhospitable grey rocky peaks, there was a high valley flowing with water and backed by terraced fields rich with fruit and vegetables. The kafeneon proprietor told us of a great place to stay.

View Out The Picture Window

It's worth all the trouble to find a remote house if the adjacent road accommodates camels. Who wouldn't trade a suburban view of lawns and cars for these ungainly beasts with their air of vast superiority and aloofness? That was the unexpected extra added to a "stopping-awhile" house where we watched and listened to a camel train flowing past, with the beasts fearfully belching.

We went to watch the parade at the first sound of a growling rumble. We listened dumfounded at the last blat of the lips. "Humans!" they complained, "are both insignificant and disgusting. That! (and here came the sound) to them."

Heating The Unheatable

But, out of season, be certain to check the heating arrangements, although the local people will swear none is needed. Some friends rented a house on the Spanish coast and were assured that heating was no problem. "Look at the palm trees and oleander bushes in bloom. This is a tropical climate."

Our friends had to purchase two portable bottle-gas heaters and a huge electric hearth to keep them going through a long and black winter. At the end of six months they had spent little on rent but a bundle on heating.

With the assurance that heating isn't really necessary you will visit Spanish families on the Mediterranean coast who greet one at the door wearing padded, floor length house coats that would look appropriate on Eskimos. They invite you to sit at the dining table for a visit. The insulated table cloth is lifted, knees push under, feet are rested on a wooden platform near but not quite touching the red hot charcoal brazier glowing underneath. There will be a normal conversation going on with remarks about the "unusual" weather.

Moving Day

After "stopping awhile" it's time to move on. You pack up and put things away in the van; you sell or give away the extra furnishings and return the little house to its former nakedness. You say goodbye to neighbors and new friends who, for a time, welcomed you as one of them. And then the questions begin: "Why go? Why not stay here where we are welcome, where fruits are ripening, where every corner has become familiar and. . . ." No matter all the good, golden times you've had, you bang the door shut and step out once more. "Stopping awhile" was good, yet the thought of open skies, changing vistas, fresh faces, new languages, new costumes, new travels heats your blood. There will be plenty of time to settle down when you finally hang up your walking shoes and return to reminisce. Right now the time has come again to seek adventures.

EPILOGUE: WHEN DO YOU STOP?

People ask us all the time: when will you stop Gypsying? Or, when will you get bored with so much freedom? When will you return to. . .well, you know, life as usual?

Gypsying and all it has to teach us won't evaporate; in this sense we hope never to "go back" or "stop." We don't ever want to be fooled by TIME again. We don't want yesterdays filled with regret; nor do we want anxious tomorrows. We've found and are determined to hold on to the freedom to center on each precious moment.

Of course we will return home to our house and neighborhood and finally stay put. . . .at least for a while. Yet we have learned that the only true, satisfying Home lies in the heart. So now, as it happens, we can be at-home anywhere as long as our heart is clear about its priorities.

We've changed our attitude towards a lot of things but especially about people. Friends are more important to us than ever before, and we are more open to forming new friendships. Idle entertainments don't attract us much any more because they don't hold a candle to the full-blooded adventures that we know await us. We don't ever want to "retire" in the usual sense of withdrawing from the action, from work which connects us to the world. We are not attracted to a life of total leisure and constant play; the boredom would doom us. Work goes with us: writing, sketching, maintaining our traveling home, correspondence, discovering new ideas, new experiences, new art. Or more accurately, work and play and learning get mixed together in the yeasty dough we know as the Gypsy Life.

We won't stop Gypsying. Curiosity and a passion for what lies over the horizon keeps us on the move. Imagine what each of us has yet to experience! That is why we invite you to come with us! Let's leave the house, shut the door, climb into a camper and start down the open road with all the wide world before us.

TOURIST OFFICES IN THE UNITED STATES

BELGIUM

Belgium National Tourist Office
745 Fifth Avenue
New York, New York 10022

EGYPT

A.R.E. Tourist Office
630 Fifth Avenue
New York, New York 10020

323 Geary Street
San Francisco, California 94102

FRANCE

French Government Tourist Office
9401 Wilshire Blvd., Suite 314
Beverly Hills, California 90212

645 N. Michigan Avenue
Chicago, Illinois 60611

610 Fifth Avenue
New York, New York 10020

323 Geary Street
San Francisco, California 94102

GREECE

Greek National Trust Organization
168 N. Michigan Avenue
Chicago, Illinois 60601

611 West 6th Street
Los Angeles, California 90017

645 Fifth Avenue
New York, New York 10022

2211 Massachusetts Avenue, N.W.
Washington, D. C. 20008

GREAT BRITAIN

British Tourist Authority
John Hancock Center, Suite 3320
875 N. Michigan Avenue
Chicago, Illinois 60611

612 S. Flower Street
Los Angeles, California 90017

40 W. 57th St.
New York, New York 10019

ISRAEL

Israel Government Tourist Office
Empire State Building
350 Fifth Avenue
New York, New York 10118

5 S. Wabash Avenue
Chicago, Illinois 60603

4151 Southwest Freeway
Houston, Texas 77027

6380 Wilshire Boulevard
Los Angeles, California 90048

ITALY

Italian Government Travel Office
500 N. Michigan Avenue
Chicago, Illinois 60611

630 Fifth Avenue
New York, New York 10020

360 Post Street
San Francisco, California 94119

MOROCCO

Morocco Tourist Office
20 E. 46th St.
New York, New York 10017

Suite 3762
2049 Century Park East
Los Angeles, California 90067

NETHERLANDS

Netherlands Information Service
City Hall
Holland, Michigan 49423

Netherlands National Tourist Office
437 Madison Avenue
New York, New York 10036

605 Market Street
San Francisco, California 94104

PORTUGAL

Portuguese National Tourist Office
The Palmer House
17 E. Monroe Street, Room 500
Chicago, Illinois 60603

1 Park Plaza, Suite 1305
3250 Wilshire Boulevard
Los Angeles, California 90010

548 Fifth Avenue
New York, New York 100368

SPAIN

Spanish National Tourist Office
Suite 915 East
845 N. Michigan Avenue
Chicago, Illinois 60611

665 Fifth Avenue
New York, New York 10022

Hypolita and St. George Streets
St. Augustine, Florida 32084

1 Hallidie Plaza
San Francisco, California 94123

SWITZERLAND

Swiss National Tourist Office
104 S. Michigan Avenue
Chicago, Illinois 60603

608 Fifth Avenue
New York, New York 10020

250 Stockton Street
San Francisco, California 94105

TUNISIA (None in US)

Tunisian Tourist Office
29/30 St. James Street
London SW1, England

TURKEY

A.B.D./U.S.A.
821 United Nations Plaza
New York, New York 10036

YUGOSLAVIA

Yugoslav National Tourist Office
630 Fifth Avenue, Suite 210
New York, New York 10020

APPENDIX B

MONEY MATTERS

We think it wise for a person bent on becoming a Gypsy traveler to read some economic theory and economic news. We especially like:

The Inflation Crisis and
  How to Resolve It
Henry Hazlitt
Arlington House

Inflation-Proofing Your Investments
Harry Browne
Warner Books

The weekly magazine, "The Economist", provides broad and fair coverage of international economic and political news as well as insights into the changing values of foreign currencies. Available at European newsstands and in large cities in N. Africa and the Middle East.

For U.S. subscriptions, write to:

The Economist
P.O. Box 904
Farmingdale, N. Y. 11737-9804

To understand Swiss banking:

The Complete Guide to Swiss Banks
Harry Browne Special Reports
Box 5586B
Austin, Texas 78763

CURRENCY

Country	Currency Unit	Subunit
Belgium	franc	centime
Britain	pound	pence
Egypt	pound	piastre
France	franc	centime
Greece	drachma	
Holland	guilder	cent
Israel	shekel	agorot
Italy	lira	
Morocco	dirham	
Portugal	escudo	
Spain	peseta	centimo
Switzerland	franc	centime
Tunisia	dinar	millime
Turkey	lira	
Yugoslavia	dinar	para

APPENDIX C

AVERAGE TEMPERATURES
(Fahrenheit)

	Maximum/Minimum	
	February	August
EGYPT, Cairo (Day-Night Ave.)	59	86
ENGLAND, London	44/35	72/55
FRANCE, Paris	46/32	75/54
GREECE, Athens	55/43	95/73
ISRAEL, Jerusalem	65/48	82/66
ITALY, Rome	55/41	86/66
MOROCCO, Marrakesch	64/41	100/68
NETHERLANDS, Amsterdam	43/30	70/54
PORTUGAL, Lisbon	55/48	76/66
SPAIN, Madrid	52-35	86/63
SWITZERLAND, Geneva	37/28	70/59
TUNISIA, Tunis	55/43	95/73
YUGOSLAVIA, Split	5 ¼ 1	85/71

This Data is supplied by the tourist offices of the countries. Our experience tells us to add ten degrees fahrenheit to winter temperatures for a better approximation.
Since all European temperatures will be expressed in Centigrade, or more correctly, Celsius, you convert thus: $C + 17.8 \times 1.8 = F$

APPENDIX D

GETTING AROUND CHEAPLY

LOW COST FLIGHTS

1. Student Flights: Since more and more older people have enrolled as fulltime students in colleges, it is possible to obtain a Council on International Student Identity Card as long as you can produce proof of enrollment. You're too old for discounts in Europe, but charter flights sponsored by CIEE are plentiful to Europe. Send for this year's Student Work Study Travel Catalog:

CIEE
205 East 42nd Street
New York, NY 10017

CIEE
1093 Broxton Avenue
Los Angeles, California 90024

CIEE
312 Sutter Street
San Francisco, California 94108

Check with International Students Travel Conference or CIEE office at the nearest university.

2. Transamerica Airline: Call them at (800) 223-7402 for ticket prices to Ireland and Holland.

SURFACE TRAVEL IN EUROPE: (Until you've found your Gypsy wagon.)

1. Buses are generally the cheapest way to travel in Spain, because most bus lines are heavily subsidized.

2. Britrail and Eurailpasses, from 15-day to 3-month passes can be bought only in the U. S. for unlimited travel in Europe. For someone on the 22- city-in-15-days tour they are fine. But the temptation to go-go-go is too great. You save money but work yourself into a frazzle. If you insist, see your travel agent.

3. Over-night, second class rail trips, especially out of the high summer season can be pleasant and inexpensive. You sleep in a little bunk called a couchette and share the compartment with five others for about $8 more than the cost of your ticket. This saves you the cost of a hotel.

FERRYBOAT TRAVEL

No matter how you travel, you will undoubtedly use at least one ferryboat. The ABC Shipping Guide, issued monthly, provides the most comprehensive and accurate information. Go to a travel agency in Europe to see a copy. Or, you can order one from:

ABC Travel Guides Ltd.
Oldhill, London Road,
Dunstable, Bedfordshire
England

APPENDIX E

RENTING AND BUYING YOUR GYPSY HOME

CAMPER VANS

To rent a camper van in England, contact one of the following:

Apex Leisure Hire
64 Albert Embankment
London SE1 7TP
Tel: 01·735 5956

John Grooms Association
for the Disabled
10 Gloucester Drive
Finsbury Park
London N4 2LP
Tel: 01·802 7272

London Motor Caravans
(Hammersmith) Ltd
302/306 King Street
Hammersmith
London W6 9NH
Tel: 01·741 0552

Motorhome Rentals (Europe) Ltd
Lowood Garage
12 Kings Avenue
Clapham
London SW4
Tel: 01·720 6492 or 6721

Southern Cross Campers Ltd
Motor Caravan Centre
Pantiles Park
London Road
Bagshot GU19 5HN
Tel: Bagshot (0276) 75056 or 73861

Stevens Motorhome Holidays
88·90 High Street
Hampton Hill
Twickenham, Middlesex
TW12 1PA
Tel: 01·977 2117

Testwood Motors (Car Hire) Ltd
331 Salisbury Road
Totton
Southhampton SO4 3ZU
Tel: Totton (0703) 865727

To purchase a van, contact your local Volkswagen or Mercedes agency for a brochure on the Westfalia conversions. Ask about the diesel models of the VW 2.8L model or the Mercedes 207D model. They can be picked up at the factory or delivered to an airport. In England, PI Motorhomes in Poole makes a large selection of cab·over campers on Ford Transit chassis, available in diesel. There are several smaller truck converters in England that use General Motors Bedford chassis; ask the British Tourist Authority for the current list. Or, take the poor·man's route and walk to the front of Australia House in London and take your pick from the "curb market". Caution: insist on a left·hand drive unit for Europe.

Once you own a van you can store it at:

Calvers Caravan Storage
Woodland's Park Road
Clapham, Bedford MK 416 EJ
England
Tel: (0234) 595 84

CANAL BOATS

For the biggest agency with boats based at canal ports both in England and in Europe, contact:

Blake's Holidays Ltd.
Wroxham, Norwich NR12 8DH
England
Tel. 60 53 3585

To contact their booking agents:

Bargain Boating
Morgantown Travel Service
127 High Street
Morgantown, West Virginia 26505
Tel: (304) 292-8471

Bonanza Travel Service Inc.
3952 West Touhy Avenue
Lincolnwood, Illinois 60645
Tel: (312) 674-3770 also
(312) 583-7800

Canals Europe
220 Redwood Highway
Mill Valley, California 94941

Boat Enquiries
43 Botley Road
Oxford OX2 OPT, England
Tel. (0865) 727288

SAIL BOATS

Charter companies change quickly, appear and disappear so that no listing can be current. English charter companies have boats in England and on the Continent. "Yachting Monthly" is available on newsstands in England and major cities in Europe or by subscription. It is the best place to find second-hand sail boats, lists of yacht brokers and qualified instruction in sailing, pilotage and navigation.

Yachting Monthly
Subscription Services
Heyward's Heath
West Sussex, England

Recommended yacht brokers:

England Martin Bandey
13a Southern Road
Southhampton 503 3ES
Tel: (04218) 4705

Spain David Morgan
Edificio Bahia
Ciudad Ibiza
(Balleares)

Holland Robert Bootz
Oud Loosdrechtsedijk 169A
1231 LV Loosdrecht
Tel: (02158) 1507

HORSE-DRAWN CARAVANS

Irish Tourist Board
757 Third Avenue
New York, N. Y. 10017
Tel: (212) 418-0800

APPENDIX F

CLUBS, MAPS AND DIRECTORIES

AUTO CLUBS

Great Britain's two automobile clubs are super organizations run on the premise that motoring is still a sport. They provide maps, advice on trips, insurance and much more.

Royal Automobile Club
49 Pall Mall
London SWIY 5HW
Tel: (01) 839 7050

Automobile Association
Fanum House
Basingstoke, Hampshire
RG21 2EA
Tel: (0256) 20123

CAMPING ASSOCIATIONS

Europe is full of camping associations, but the most useful ones are in England.

The Caravan Club
East Grinstead House
East Grinstead
West Sussex RH19 1UA
Tel: (0342) 26944

The Motor Caravanner's Club
52 Wolseley Road
London N8 8RP
Tel: (01) 340 5865

The U.S. National Campers & Hikers Association Inc. is especially helpful since it is affiliated with International Federation of Camping and Caravaning (FICC). As a member, you can get the Carnet-Camping International card which entitles you to reduced rates at many private campgrounds in Europe. It also includes "Third Party" insurance. Membership $10. Carnet $4.

National Campers & Hikers Association Inc.
7172 Transit Road
Buffalo, New York 14221
Tel: (716) 634-5433

American Youth Hostels is the U. S. branch of the international organization that provides the cheapest beds in 5000 hostels around the world. You're eligible for a Senior Pass if over 18 or a Senior Citizen Pass if 60 or over.

American Youth Hostels Inc.
1332 I Street N. W., Suite 800
Washington, D. C. 20005
Tel: (800) 424-9426

CANAL CHARTS

BELGIUM

Ministerie Van Openbare Werken
Exploitatiedienst de Scheepvaartwegen
Residence Palace 4e Verdieping
Westraat 155
B-1040 Brussel
Belgium

Prins Boudewijnlaan 35
B-2700 Sint Niklass
Belgium

Ministere des Travaux Publics
rue de la Loi 155
1040 Bruxelles

FRANCE

For general information and rules contact the French Tourist Office [See Appendix A] and ask for "Yachting and Boating in French Waters".

The best charts for French Canals provide such detailed information that you can locate even food markets, telephones and engine repair shops. They have French, English, and German legends and can be obtained from:

Carte-Guide de Navigation Fluviale
Editions Cartoghraphiques Maritimes
56 rue de l'Universite
75007 Paris

GREAT BRITAIN

If you rent a canal boat, all cruising instructions come with the boat. Stanford Maritime publishes two books that cover the main canals and rivers: Inland Cruising Map and Stanford's River Thames Map.

NETHERLANDS

For the Netherlands there are excellent, detailed charts produced by:

Netherlands Wateroeristiche Board ANWB
5 Museumplein, Amsterdam

Or the ANWB waterkaart can be obtained in ANWB offices in any Dutch city or from yacht chandlers.

MAPS

In Europe maps cost money. In the U.S. you may still be able to get free oil company maps of Europe.

Shell Touring Service
P.O. Box 538
Comfort, Texas 78013

Exxon Touring Service
1251 Avenue of Americas
New York, New York 10020

Book stores in Europe sell maps. But if you want superior maps for that desert trek or a climb in the Atlas Mountains try the Edward Stanford Ltd. cartographers in London.

Edward Stanford Ltd.
12-14
Long Acre
London WC2
Tel: (01) 836 1321

This store is like a gourmet restaurant for travelers. Sample the 200 plus pieces of the International World Map. Or the A.M.S. Topo World series of U502 of India and Pakistan with details of the Himalayas!

EUROPE AND THE MEDITERRANEAN MAP SERIES

For Southern Europe:

Carte Michelin
46 Ave. de Breteuil
75341 Paris

For Italy, Switzerland and Germany:

Roger Lascelles
3 Holland Park Mansions
16 Holland Park Gardens
London W14 8DY
Tel: (01) 603 8489

CAMPING DIRECTORIES

The best directories are available from tourist offices or at border stations. They list major campgrounds. None are comprehensive since private campgrounds often do not advertise, and some of these are the very best available. Other good directories include:

All About Camping in Europe
Hall Schell
Rajo Publications
P. O. Box 1014
Grass Valley, California 94945

European Camping and Caravaning
Bob & Claudette Cope
Drake Publishers, New York; 1974

Europa Camping and Caravaning
Recreational Equipment, Inc.
1525 11th Avenue
Seattle, Washington 98122

APPENDIX G

COMMUNICATIONS

MAIL SERVICE

British Monomarks
London WC1N 3XX
England
Tel: (01) 405 0463

Ask for a brochure that outlines their services.

RADIO

British Broadcasting Company
World Service
P. O. Box 76
Bush House
London WC2B 4PH
England

Write them for a free copy of "London Calling" the monthly program guide.

APPENDIX H

TRAVEL GUIDEBOOKS

A really good guidebook opens the door to unanticipated opportunities. Two series are standard for most of Southern Europe. The first is the *Michelin Red and Green Guides* to hotels, restaurants and sights. The other is the *Norton Blue Guides*; they offer unusually detailed information on archaeology, the arts, architecture and history.

OTHER RECOMMENDED TRAVEL GUIDES

Harvard Student Agencies: *Let's Go* series.

A Money-Wise Guide to the Lands and Islands of the Mediterranean
Michael Von Haag
Travelaid Services Ltd.
63 Old Town
London SW4

The Arthur Frommer Guides are the best-selling continental guidebooks and deserve their success. Frommer sets out to tell where and how to go on a fixed budget per day. In addition to his *Europe on $?? a Day* (amount changes every year or so), Frommer's *Dollarwise Guides* cover most countries.

Recommended unique guides from John Muir Publications include:

Europe Through the Back Door, by Rick Steves
Europe 101, by Rick Steves
Asia Through The Back Door, by Rick Steves and John Gottberg
The Traveler's Guide To Asian Culture, by John Gottberg
The People's Guide To Mexico, by Carl Franz
The People's Guide To Camping In Mexico, by Carl Franz

John Muir Publications
P.O. Box 613
Santa Fe, New Mexico 87504
(See Order Form in back of this book.)

We give five stars to:

The Art and Adventure of Traveling Cheaply (An insider's guide to the ins and outs of going anywhere in the world on next to nothing):

Rich Berg
And/Or Press
Box 2246
Berkeley, California 94702

THE CRAFT OF SAILING AND CANAL CRUISING

Most mariners get their start by reading about the exploits of others. There are dozens of books in this field, good for dreaming. We recommend:

Eric Hiscock (The king of international sailors)

Voyaging Under Sail, Oxford University Press, 1970
Cruising Under Sail, Oxford University Press, 1981
Sou'west in Wanderer IV, Sheridan, 1986

Lyn and Larry Pardey (the heirs apparent)

Cruising in Seraffyn, Seven Seas, 1976
Seraffyn's Mediterranean Adventure, Norton, 1981
The Self-Sufficient Sailor, Norton, 1982

Several good books on canal cruising are available. We recommend these publishers who will supply you with their catalogues.

Adlard Coles
Granada Publishing Ltd.
8 Grafton St.
London W1X 3LA
Tel: (01) 493 7070

Stanford Maritime Ltd.
12-14 Long Acre
London WC 2E 9LP
Tel: (01) 836 7863

David & Charles
P. O. Box 257
North Pomfret, Vermont 05053
Tel: (800) 423-4525

APPENDIX I

U.S. CUSTOMS REGULATIONS

Since you may return to the states with an armful of cherished junk, familiarize yourself with customs regulations.

U. S. Customs Service
P.O. Box 7407
Washington, D.C. 20229

Ask for:

"Know Before You Go"
"Importing a Car"*
"Customs Hints For Returning U. S. Residents"

*It is very difficult to import a car into the U.S. No foreign car can be imported unless it is manufactured specifically for the U. S. Go directly to the manufacturer to obtain all the details before you buy a car to bring back with you.

APPENDIX J

SCHOOLS

Alice Fleming, *A Complete Guide to Accredited Correspondence Schools*, Doubleday, Garden City, NJ, 1980.

John Arthur Garraty, *New Guide to Study Abroad*, Harper & Row, New York, NY, 1981.

J.K. Sargent, *Schools Abroad*, Porter Sargent Publishers, Boston, MA, 1985.

Peterson's Guide to Independent Secondary Schools, Peterson's Guide, Princeton, NJ, latest addition.

UNESCO, *Study Abroad*, Paris, 1983.

INDEX

JMP TRAVELERS CATALOG

All Items Field Tested, Highly Recommended, Completely Guaranteed and Discounted Below Retail.

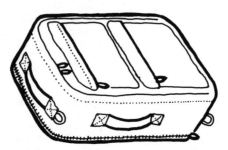

Combination Rucksack/
Suitcase . . . . $70.00 postpaid

At 9"x 21"x 13", this specially designed, sturdy, functional bag is maximum carry-on-the-plane size. (Fits under the seat.) Constructed by Jesse Ltd. of rugged waterproof nylon Cordura material, with hide-away shoulder straps, waist belt (for use as a ruck sack) and top and side handles and a detachable shoulder strap (for toting as a suitcase). Perimeter zippers allow easy access to the roomy (2200 cu. in.) central compartment. Two small outside pockets are perfect for maps and other frequently used items. Two thousand JMP Travelers took these bags around the world last year and returned satisfied. Comparable bags cost much more. If you're looking for maximum "carry-on size" and a suitcase that can be converted into a back pack, this is your best bet. Available in navy blue, black, gray or burgundy.

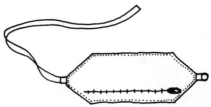

Money Belt . . . . $8.95 postpaid

Required! Ultra-light, sturdy, under-the-pants, nylon pouch just big enough to carry the essentials comfortably. We never travel without one and hope you won't either. Beige, nylon zipper, one size fits all, with instructions.

Qty.	Title	Each	Total
	Alaska in 22 Days - *Lanier* (March '88)	$ 6.95	
	American Southwest in 22 Days - *Harris* (April '88)	6.95	
	Australia in 22 Days - *Gottberg*	6.95	
	China in 22 Days - *Duke & Victor*	6.95	
	Europe in 22 Days - *Steves*	6.95	
	Germany, Austria & Switzerland in 22 Days - *Steves*	6.95	
	Great Britain in 22 Days - *Steves*	6.95	
	India in 22 Days - *Mathur* (April '88)	6.95	
	Japan in 22 Days - *Old*	6.95	
	Mexico in 22 Days - *Rogers & Rosa*	6.95	
	Norway, Denmark & Sweden in 22 Days - *Steves*	6.95	
	West Indies in 22 Days - *Morreale*	6.95	
	All-Suite Hotel Guide - *Lanier*	9.95	
	Asia 101 - *Gottberg* (March '88)	11.95	
	Asia Through the Back Door - *Steves & Gottberg*	11.95	
	Complete Guide to Bed & Breakfasts - *Lanier*	12.95	
	Elegant Small Hotels - *Lanier*	12.95	
	Europe 101 - *Steves*	11.95	
	Europe Through the Back Door - *Steves*	11.95	
	Gypsying After 40 - *Harris*	12.95	
	Heart of Jerusalem - *Nellhaus* (Feb. '88)	12.95	
	Mona Winks - *Steves* (April '88)	9.95	
	People's Guide to Camping in Mexico - *Franz* (April '88)	11.95	
	People's Guide to Mexico - *Franz*	13.95	

		Subtotal	$
Non-U.S. payments must be in		Shipping	$ 1.75
U.S. funds drawn on a U.S. bank.		**Total enclosed**	$

METHOD OF PAYMENT (CHECK ONE)

☐ Charge to my (circle one): MasterCard VISA AmEx
☐ Check or Money Order Enclosed (Sorry, no CODs or Cash)
Credit Card Number

Expiration Date ☐☐ — ☐☐

Signature _____

Required for Credit Card Purchases

Telephone: Office (____) _____ Home (____) _____
Name _____
Address _____
City _____ State _____ Zip _____

Send to: John Muir Publications
P.O. Box 613 Santa Fe, NM 87504-0613
(505) 982-4078
Please allow 4-6 weeks for delivery.